Discov...
British Re...
Traditions

Ian F. W. Beckett

British Library Cataloguing in Publication Data: Beckett, I. F. W. (Ian Frederick William) Discovering British regimental traditions. – 2nd ed. – (Discovering series; no. 292) 1. Great Britain. Army – History 2. Great Britain. Army – Military life 3. Great Britain – History, Military I. Title 355.1'0941. ISBN-13: 978 0 7478 0662 2.

Front cover: (Foreground) A soldier of The Coldstream Guards with the Queen's Colour at the Changing of the Guard at Buckingham Palace in 1999. (Background top) Members of the Sealed Knot re-enacting a Civil War engagement at Old Wardour Castle, Wiltshire. (Background, bottom left) A 'Boxman' of The Life Guards at Horse Guards in Whitehall. (Background, bottom right) A painting of the 17th Lancers, who took part in the Charge of the Light Brigade at Balaclava in 1854.
Back cover: The Royal Green Jackets receiving the freedom of Aylesbury, Buckinghamshire, in 1998.
Title page: An inspection of a guard formed by The Life Guards at Horse Guards in Whitehall.

ACKNOWLEDGEMENTS

Photographs are acknowledged as follows: Michael Bass, Lime Tree Studio, Tring, pages 32 (top), 93, 94 (all), 97, 98, 106, 130; Ian Beckett, pages 18, 35 (top), 59, 75, 96 (top), 99, 100 (both), 101 (top), 102 (top right and bottom), cover (top); *Bucks Herald*, page 60 (top); Peter Duckers, page 56; Jacqueline Fearn, page 96 (bottom); Cadbury Lamb, pages 1, 6, 7, 8 (bottom), 9, 10, 12, 13, 16, 20 (bottom), 23, 24, 25 (bottom), 26, 27, 33, 37, 38, 43, 46, 49, 51, 52, 53, 57, 60 (bottom), 61, 62, 63, 68, 79 (bottom), 81, 83 (bottom), 86, 88, 92, 101 (bottom), 102 (top left), 103, 104, 105 (both), 109, 110, 111, 112, 116, 117, 119, 124, 125, cover (foreground and bottom left); *The Soldier,* page 78.

The drawings of badges on pages 42 (top), 48 (bottom), 55 (bottom), 71, 72 and 73 (bottom) are by Edward Stamp. The illustrations on pages 11, 14, 17, 19, 20 (top), 30, 34, 40, 42 (bottom), 44, 47, 50, 58, 65, 67, 70, 73 (top), 77, 80, 89, 90 and 95 (both) are from *The Illustrated London News.* The illustrations on pages 8 (top), 21, 22, 28, 29, 32, 35 (bottom), 36 (bottom), 39 (both), 45, 54, 55 (top), 66 (bottom), 69, 74, 82, 85, 87 (both) and 91 are from old postcards.

Published in 2007 by Shire Publications Ltd, Cromwell House, Church Street, Princes Risborough, Buckinghamshire HP27 9AA, UK. (Website: www.shirebooks.co.uk)
Copyright © 1999 and 2007 by Ian F. W. Beckett. First published 1999. Second edition 2007, revised and including colour illustrations. Number 292 in the Discovering series. ISBN 978 0 7478 0662 2.
Ian F. W. Beckett is hereby identified as the author of this work in accordance with Section 77 of the Copyright, Designs and Patents Act, 1988.

Printed in Malta by Gutenberg Press Ltd, Gudja Road, Tarxien PLA19, Malta.

Contents

A soldier of a Territorial battalion of the King's Own Scottish Borderers during the First World War.

Introduction

Tradition is a problematic concept, which some historians believe to be invariably an invention intended to inculcate particular values. However, a military tradition can be legitimately interpreted in terms of the continuities over time that become evident beyond those trends deriving simply from military conservatism. In this sense, there is most certainly a British military tradition that can be traced from the moment of the establishment of a regular standing army in peacetime in the seventeenth century. There is also an alternative and even older amateur British military tradition deriving from those forces raised locally for home defence on a systematic basis from the sixteenth century, but with origins in the Anglo-Saxon kingdoms between the late seventh and early ninth centuries. These professional and amateur military traditions have existed alongside a tradition of popular anti-militarism, which has helped to shape the many paradoxes of what might be termed British military culture. The interplay of these conflicting traditions has resulted in remarkable continuities not only over the past three centuries of British military history, but also in terms of those military forces whose existence pre-dated the actual sanction of a standing army.

One of the most distinctive aspects of the British Army is its regimental tradition. Yet regimental tradition is often bogus in terms of continuity and certainly often spurious in terms of county lineage. There are genuinely ancient regiments, but in other cases only nicknames and customs were transmitted from one creation to another. Regiments were raised and disbanded frequently as needs dictated, with the regimental numbers given to wartime creations simply re-allocated in the next crisis. In fact, regimental county affiliation was only briefly established in 1782 and not applied systematically until 'localisation' was introduced in 1872 and then extended through 'territorialisation' in 1881. However, little logic was applied to these processes, and territorialisation certainly did not imply that a county regiment recruited exclusively or even primarily from its parent county.

It is a system that has also been frequently criticised, but it was a better answer to the requirements of a global empire than continental-style corps and divisions. Moreover, it has been one of the principal factors that has maintained morale in conditions in which that of other armies collapsed. In the First World War, for example, the rallying call of Lieutenant Colonel Elstob on 21st March 1918 ('The Manchester Regiment will hold Manchester Hill to the last') and the notice in Mansel Copse cemetery on the Somme ('The Devons held this trench, the Devons hold it still') are essentially British in their expression. Increasingly in the twentieth century, however, the regimental system has come under threat from, firstly, the demands of mass modern warfare between 1914 and 1945 and, secondly, the effects of the military technological revolution since 1945. Combined arms battlegroups are now the norm in medium- and high-intensity conflict although the individual battalion remains the best structure for low-intensity conflict embracing such tasks as counter-insurgency and peacekeeping. Similarly, the identity of former specialist corps has been significantly reduced by the creation of two large multi-purpose units, the **Adjutant General's Corps** and the **Royal Logistic Corps**, in 1992 and 1993 respectively while the successive series of amalgamations since 1958 has resulted in the creation of ever larger regiments, in which individual battalions have represented more and more collective traditions of those long vanished. It has also been argued that the persistence of what might be termed regimental politics, not least in terms of campaigns to save individual regiments or battalions, has made the army less able to defend itself collectively against the continuing process of reduction.

Indeed, technological change combined with socio-economic pressures may altogether undermine the continuing viability of the regimental system, a new wave of amalgamations taking place in 2006 and 2007 which, *inter alia*, swept away the last regiments left untouched since their original establishment, namely The Royal Scots (1633), The Green Howards (1600) and The Cheshire Regiment (1609). That would be a pity for, whether invented or not, the custom and ritual of tradition are an essential ingredient as much of institutional identity as of national identity. Without a sense of the past, there can be no understanding of the present and no basis on which to model the future. At a time of some uncertainty in terms of the army's future size and functions, it is appropriate to recall the extraordinary past of an institution which has served the country so well for over 300 years. As Field Marshal Lord Birdwood wrote in 1942, 'Let us preserve our British regimental traditions with all our care, and cherish their separate glories, for they are a precious part of our heritage ..... Men live for them, and small as they may seem, will die for them.'

Note: The titles of existing regiments and corps are shown in the text in bold type.

Members of the King's Troop, Royal Horse Artillery, in Green Park.

1. The Regular Army

There is some room for debate as to whether the precise origins of the modern British Army lie in the creation of Parliament's New Model Army in 1644, the restoration of an organised royal army in 1660, or the establishment of the army fully under parliamentary control in 1689 following the Glorious Revolution. Technically, however, there was no British Army prior to the Act of Union between England (which had effectively incorporated Wales by acts of 1536 and 1543) and Scotland in 1707.

Of course, the English Crown had long employed professional soldiers as part of the royal household. The rulers of pre-Conquest England, for example, maintained royal bodyguards such as the *housecarls* particularly associated with Cnut (1016-35). Following the Norman Conquest, medieval English kings were similarly served by the knights of the household or *familia* together with their squires and followers. Indeed, King Edward I (1272-1307) is said to have had almost 700 cavalry attached to his household in the thirteenth century, and the household remained the core of armies raised through feudal and other obligations for campaigns in Wales, Scotland and France. The Crown also routinely employed mercenaries and, from the thirteenth century, entered contractual arrangements with its own magnates. Indeed, medieval armies were raised by a bewildering variety of methods, including occasional recourse to levies.

A more systematic organisation began to emerge in the late fifteenth and sixteenth centuries. This was marked not only by the development of a national militia in the mid sixteenth century and a more general reliance upon levies but also by that of permanent standing regular garrisons in key fortresses such as Berwick, Carlisle, Dover and Calais. At the same time, in imitation of the Scottish archers who acted as a royal bodyguard in France, the Yorkist kings raised a 200-strong body of archers as a palace guard. Following his victory over the last Yorkist king at Bosworth, Henry VII (1485-1509) established the similar **Yeomen of the Guard** in 1486. Seen still on

Guarding the 'gateway to England', Dover Castle housed one of the first permanent regular garrisons before the establishment of a formal standing army.

The Yeomen of the Guard being inspected at St James's Palace prior to the State Opening of Parliament.

state occasions in their distinctive Tudor dress, the Yeomen of the Guard should not be confused with the **Yeomen Warders** of the Tower of London, who are an entirely separate body. Whereas the duties of the Yeomen Warders were always confined to the Tower, the Yeomen of the Guard formerly accompanied the monarch even on to the battlefield, the last occasion being when King George II (1727-60) com-

manded his army at the battle of Dettingen during the War of Austrian Succession in 1743. Yeomen of the Guard also still have the duty of searching the vaults of the Palace of Westminster before the state opening of Parliament to ensure no repetition of the Gunpowder Plot (1605). In the reign of Henry VIII (1509-47), a further small body of mounted men armed with poleaxes was formed as an inner guard in 1509, but also as a cadre of young aristocratic officers in the event of a war. Originally known as the Gentlemen Pensioners, they have survived as the **Honourable Corps of Gentlemen at Arms**. Now fulfilling a similar ceremonial role to the Yeomen of the Guard on state occasions, they wear a uniform designed by William IV (1830-7) modelled on that of contemporary dragoons. The **Royal Company of Archers of Scotland**, which is the sovereign's household bodyguard in Scotland, was instituted in 1677 although it does not formally appear in the Army List.

Under Elizabeth I (1558-1603) those armies sent to Ireland, France and the Netherlands were raised

A Yeoman Warder of the Tower of London. Unlike the Yeomen of the Guard, Yeomen Warders take no part in Court duties.

Members of the English Civil War Society in New Model Army uniform at the Festival of History, Kelmarsh, Northamptonshire, in 2006.

both by levy and by appeals to quasi-feudalism. At the time of the threat from the Spanish Armada in 1588, for example, the 45,000 men assigned as the Queen's personal army were raised by the clergy and from the personal retainers of the nobility and gentry. Under the threat from Spain, indeed, perhaps 100,000 men were drawn into Elizabethan armies for overseas service in the 1580s and 1590s. Similarly, levies were imposed for the unsuccessful French expeditions mounted by Charles I (1625-49) in the 1620s and for the Bishops' Wars in Scotland in 1639 and 1640. In the First Civil War (1642-5) King and Parliament raised 'marching armies' initially at least from volunteers but increasingly by impressment. In 1640 the Crown's standing forces had been no more than about 1000 men, but at the height of the Civil War there were perhaps 110,000 men under arms in England, and in January 1645 Parliament created its New Model Army of 22,000 men, exclusive of supernumeraries and other provincial forces. The New Model consisted of eleven regiments of horse, one of dragoons, twelve of foot and an artillery train protected by an additional two regiments of foot. The victory of the New Model and the establishment of the Cromwellian protectorate ushered in what had the appearance of a military regime although, in fact, the army was reduced in size and mostly employed, after the subjugation of Scotland and Ireland, in overseas campaigns such as the seizure of Jamaica in 1655 and Dunkirk in 1657.

With the restoration of Charles II (1660-85) the New Model was largely disbanded while the detached New Model garrison at Dunkirk was initially merged with Charles's own army of exiled royalists. When Dunkirk was sold back to the French in 1662, the former New Model regiments were posted safely away to Tangier, which had passed to Charles as part of the wedding dowry of his queen, Catherine of Braganza. Two units of the New Model survived to be taken into royal service in 1661. The regiment of foot of the architect of the restoration, General George Monck, became the Lord General's Regiment of Foot Guards, later the **Coldstream Guards**. Originally raised in 1650, it was thus senior to the King's Royal Regiment of Guards or 1st Foot Guards, later the **Grenadier Guards**, which was the regiment of exiled royalists known as Wentworth's Regiment, formed in 1656. Technically, therefore, the Coldstream were the 2nd Foot Guards but, in deference to their greater antiquity, continued to insist that this was not the case, hence their motto, *Nulli secundus* ('Second to none'). In deference to their republican origins, they do not have

9

A detachment of the Household Cavalry Mounted Regiment escorting the royal coach at the Queen's Jubilee Parade, 2002.

a royal colonel-in-chief and do not drink the loyal toast, although this latter practice was common to at least eleven regiments for varying reasons.

The second New Model unit to survive was Cromwell's former Life Guard of Horse, which was incorporated into the Royal Regiment of Horse in 1661, later the Royal Regiment of Horse Guards (The Blues) and Royal Horse Guards. As with the foot, exiled royalists formed troops of Life Guards, originally designated both Horse Guards and Horse Grenadier Guards. Later the 1st and 2nd Life Guards, they merged in 1922 as **The Life Guards**. Additional units were then raised for service in Tangier. The first was The Tangier Regiment of Foot, later successively designated the 2nd Foot and The Queen's Royal Regiment (West Surrey) and now forming part of the 1st Battalion, **The Princess of Wales's Royal Regiment (Queen's and Royal Hampshires)**. The other was the Tangier Horse, later successively designated the King's Own Royal Regiment of Dragoons, the 1st (Royal) Regiment of Dragoons and the Royal Dragoons. In 1969 the Royal Horse Guards and the Royal Dragoons were amalgamated as **The Blues and Royals**. They and **The Life Guards** still technically exist as separate entities, but since 1992 they have been considered as a single unit from which a tank regiment, **The Household Cavalry Regiment**, and a ceremonial regiment, **The Household Cavalry Mounted Regiment**, are drawn.

The new royal army numbered in theory no more than 8452 guards and garrisons in 1663 and still only 8865 in 1685. However, the actual size had been increased substantially during the Anglo-Dutch Wars, while the armies in Scotland and Ireland were on an entirely separate establishment and there was also an Anglo-Dutch Brigade permanently on loan to the Netherlands from 1674 until 1689. The latter included the Holland Regiment, later designated the 3rd Foot, The Buffs (Royal East Kent Regiment) and now forming part of the 1st Battalion, **The Princess of Wales's Royal Regiment (Queen's and Royal Hampshires)**. Two units of Scottish origin first taken on to the establishment during Charles II's reign in 1662 and 1678 respectively were His Majesty's Royal Regiment of Foot, later the 1st Foot and The Royal Scots (The Royal Regiment), and The Royal Regiment of Scots Dragoons, later The Royal Scots Greys, now forming part of **The Royal Scots Dragoon Guards**

(Carabiniers and Greys).

Under James II (1685-9) there was an even more substantial increase in the army of five new regiments of horse, two of dragoons and nine of foot, raising considerable fears about the possibility of military despotism and the enforced restitution of Catholicism. As a result, William of Orange, who was married to James's Protestant daughter, Mary, was invited to take the throne. The consequence of the flight of James II and the subsequent Glorious Revolution of 1688-9 was the imposition of firmer Parliamentary control over the army although command was still vested in the Crown. Under the Declaration of Rights, a standing army in peacetime was illegal without Parliamentary sanction while, much more significant, the army's estimates now had to be presented annually for Parliamentary approval. Although not originally intended to be part of the overall settlement, the Mutiny Act passed in 1689 also gained increasing significance as a means by which Parliament could regulate the army's internal affairs. Ironically, the accession of William and Mary (1689-1702) also effectively brought England into the mainstream of European political power conflict, necessitating large increases in the establishment during the Nine Years War (1689-97) and the War of Spanish Succession (1702-13). Thus began the cycle of wartime expansion and peacetime contraction which was henceforth to characterise the British army.

The result of this process was the continuing appearance and disappearance of wartime creations although with a steady increase of more permanent regiments of horse and foot through British participation in the War of Austrian Succession (1740-8), the Seven Years War (1756-63), the American War of Independence (1775-83) and the French Revolutionary and Napoleonic Wars (1792-1815). The 32nd Foot, for example, was raised during the War of Spanish Succession in 1702 as Edward Fox's Regiment of Foot, later becoming The Duke of Cornwall's Light Infantry and now forming part of 5th Battalion, **The Rifles**. The same regiment's 4th Battalion, disbanded in 1969, was originally the 68th Foot, later The Durham Light Infantry, a creation of the Seven Years War in 1756. The same modern regiment's 3rd Battalion, reduced in 1993, originated in 1793 as the 85th Foot (Bucks Volunteers), later

The 43rd and 52nd Foot, later the 1st and 2nd Battalions, The Oxfordshire and Buckinghamshire Light Infantry, were converted to light infantry in 1803. Both regiments distinguished themselves in the Peninsular War. At Vimiero in Portugal on 21st August 1808 the 43rd held a cemetery against four French battalions.

The Forbury Lion in Reading, Berkshire, commemorates men of the Royal Berkshire Regiment lost at Maiwand during the Second Afghan War.

2nd Battalion, The King's Shropshire Light Infantry. A considerable increase in the number of regiments on the establishment also took place as a consequence of the Indian Mutiny (1857-8) for, with the abolition of the East India Company, its nine European regiments passed to the Crown as the 102nd to 109th Foot.

Originally, regiments tended to bear the names of their colonels rather than regimental numbers since they remained very much the personal property of the colonel until the end of the eighteenth century. The 49th Foot, later 1st Battalion, The Royal Berkshire Regiment, for example, began as Trelawny's Regiment, raised from Jamaica garrison companies in 1743. The 9th Foot, later The Royal Norfolk Regiment, was Cornewall's Regiment when raised in 1685, and the 19th Foot, now **2nd Battalion, The Yorkshire Regiment (Green Howards)**, began in 1688 as Luttrell's Regiment. The process of awarding county titles as a means of assisting infantry recruiting began experimentally in 1782, but regiments much preferred the old regimental numbers and there is little evidence that it facilitated additional recruitment on the basis of county loyalty. Rather similarly, there was considerable resistance to 'localisation' in 1872 and 'territorialisation' in 1881. The former linked two regular battalions with the militia and volunteer battalions in regimental districts served by a single recruit depot. The intention was not only to draw the auxiliary forces into closer union with the regulars but also to forge a link between locality and regiment. At the same time it would also enable one regular battalion serving abroad to be supplied with reinforcing drafts from its partner at the home depot, which would be fed in turn from the recruit depot. It proved impossible to maintain equality in the number of battalions serving at home and abroad when sudden emergencies such as the Second Afghan War (1878-81) and Zulu War (1879) necessitated home battalions being hurried overseas. Moreover, while many regimental depots were in southern England, most potential recruits were in London and the industrial North and Midlands.

Nevertheless, in 1881, the linked battalions became permanently affiliated to new county regiments although, in the case of the first twenty-five regiments of foot, a second battalion was added rather than two different regiments being brought

The Royal Green Jackets maintain their link with Buckinghamshire. In 1998 they received the freedom of Aylesbury.

together. Some curious alliances were forged by localisation and territorialisation. In the case of Buckinghamshire, for example, the 16th Foot, later the 1st Battalion, The Bedfordshire and Hertfordshire Regiment and ultimately part of 3rd Battalion, **The Royal Anglian Regiment**, which disappeared in 1992, had been given the county affiliation in 1782. However, the Adjutant General, Sir Harry Calvert, was linked to a Buckinghamshire family and in 1809 switched the title to that of his own regiment, the 14th Foot. Then, in 1872 the 14th was linked to Yorkshire and in 1881 became The Prince of Wales's Own (West Yorkshire Regiment), now 1st Battalion, **the Yorkshire Regiment (Prince of Wales's Own)**. Buckinghamshire was now linked to the new county regiment formed from the 43rd and 52nd Foot, originally connected respectively with Monmouthshire and Oxfordshire, to be known as The Oxfordshire Light Infantry. In due course it became The Oxfordshire and Buckinghamshire Light Infantry in 1908 and now forms part of 2nd Battalion, **The Rifles**. However, the 43rd and 52nd continued to refer to themselves as such rather than as 1st and 2nd Battalions, The Oxfordshire Light Infantry while The Royal Bucks King's Own Militia and 1st Bucks Rifle Volunteers steadfastly refused to refer to themselves respectively as 3rd Battalion and 3rd Volunteer Battalion of The Oxfordshire Light Infantry. Similarly, the 90th Foot, originally raised in 1794 as The Perthshire Volunteers and supposedly nicknamed the Perthshire Grey-breeks from the prison breeches most were wearing when recruited, was linked with the 26th Foot, The Cameronians, originally raised in 1698 from devout Scottish Covenanters. Now after 1881 officially 2nd Battalion, The Cameronians, the 90th always referred to themselves as The Scottish Rifles. The 79th Foot, later The Queen's Own Cameron Highlanders, managed to escape possible absorption by the **Scots Guards** and remained a single-battalion regiment until 1897.

Nonetheless, territorialisation did eventually succeed in forging meaningful links between regiments and counties to the extent that the 1881 titles and connections are now fondly remembered and, on occasions, stoutly defended. An example was the vociferous public campaign to save The Argyll and Sutherland Highlanders (Princess

The 'thin red line' of the 93rd (later the 2nd Battalion, Argyll and Sutherland Highlanders) at Balaclava on 25th October 1854. Formed two deep under the command of Sir Colin Campbell, the 93rd drove off a greatly superior force of Russian cavalry.

Louise's). A union of the 91st (Princess Louise's Argyllshire Highlanders) and 93rd (The Sutherland Highlanders), the regiment was slated for disbandment in 1968 as the junior battalion in the then Highland Brigade. However, the Argylls and their flamboyant commanding officer, Lieutenant Colonel Colin Mitchell, had gained considerable national prominence for their role in restoring control of the Crater district of Aden in June 1967 after a local police mutiny in which twenty-two British servicemen had been killed. The 93rd had also been the regiment at Balaclava in October 1854 to which the famous war correspondent of *The Times*, William Russell, had referred when writing of the 'thin red line'. The regiment survived at company strength and, in 1972, was reinstated as a full battalion by the Conservative government, the party having pledged to do so while still in opposition.

2. The Auxiliary Forces

The Militia

As indicated previously, there is an 'amateur' military tradition that long pre-dates the creation of a standing army in Britain. Indeed, because the existence of a standing army was distrusted and English and British defence against invasion relied primarily on a navy, there was a distinct preference for raising temporary military or auxiliary forces only in times of crisis. The oldest of these auxiliary forces was the militia, which had its origins in the military obligations imposed on freemen in the Anglo-Saxon kingdoms such as Kent, Mercia and Wessex between the late seventh and ninth centuries. These obligations required service in times of emergency in the *fyrd*, derived from the old English word for army, selection being largely based on units of land assessment such as the hide. In some areas at least, a man was liable to serve for up to sixty days, while among the West Saxons failure to serve would result in a fine or *fyrdwite*. The concept of the fyrd survived the coming of the Normans, and it was still in existence in the twelfth century. Thereafter, the principle of emergency military service being an obligation upon the freeman was enshrined in successive medieval legislation such as the Assize of Arms (1181) and the Statute of Westminster (1285). Under the Tudors these military obligations were revived, Henry VIII even attempting to enforce the continued practice of archery as late as 1512. Moreover, under the threat of increasing tensions in Europe in the troubled reigns of Edward VI (1547-53) and Mary (1553-8), the county lieutenancy emerged and also a genuine national militia system began through the two statutes collectively known as the 1558 Militia Act. Thereafter, the militia had a formal statutory existence from 1558 to 1604, from 1648 to 1735, from 1757 to 1831 and from 1852 until 1908.

The actual basis of militia service varied considerably from period to period. Essentially it was an obligation imposed on property owners until 1757 and then a tax on manpower, with the force raised by compulsory ballot until 1831, and finally by voluntary enlistment from 1852 to the abolition of the militia in 1908. Similarly, the actual service obligation varied from period to period. In the Elizabethan period militiamen would be required to train on ten days spread throughout the year, often the four days following Easter Monday, the four following Whit Monday and two days at Michaelmas inclusive of travelling to the musters at traditional locations such as Muster Oak in Codsheath, Kent, and Muster Green in the Buttinghill Hundred of Sussex. It also became the practice after 1573 to call out only a portion of the militia for such training, those selected being known as the trained bands.

The term 'trained bands' continued in general use until 1663, and for the militia of London until 1793. Indeed, the London Trained Bands achieved a greater efficiency than many others, assisted by the periodically fashionable interest taken in martial pursuits in the City. In 1537, for example, the Guild of St George, later **The Honourable Artillery Company**, had been established to maintain 'the science and feate of shootinge' with both bows and handguns. It became the custom for the HAC, which received the 'Honourable' in 1685, to supply officers and non-commissioned officers to the London Trained Bands. It is still closely linked to the City of London, providing the Lord Mayor with an escort on civic occasions such as the annual Lord Mayor's Show on the second Saturday in November, and firing the royal salute from the Tower of London on the Sovereign's official birthday. The uniform of its Company of Pikemen and Musketeers still reflects that of the era of the Civil War, which was precipitated by the issue of whether the Crown or Parliament should control the London Trained Bands. The London Trained Bands played a significant role in mustering to deny the King entry to the capital at Turnham Green in November 1642. However, the trained bands were generally of mixed value since much depended on

The Honourable Artillery Company at the Tower of London, where it fires the royal salute on official anniversaries.

their willingness to leave their own counties, and even the London Trained Bands clamoured to return home from the Parliamentary army in April 1644.

After the Restoration the militia was revived and remained under the control of the Crown, its organisation being the task of the Lord Lieutenant in each county. The prefix 'Lord' originally derived from the rank of those who customarily filled the office and became a matter of custom. Indeed, technically there was no such office as Lord Lieutenant until the local government changes in 1974: prior to this the official title was only His or Her Majesty's Lieutenant for a particular county. Henry VII issued some commissions to individual noblemen to assume command over several counties, but the practice became more common in the reign of Edward VI, and under Elizabeth I individuals were increasingly named for single counties. The system was extended to Scotland in 1794 and to Ireland in 1831.

Some saw the militia as a constitutional alternative to a standing army, but the militia in both England and Scotland generally declined after 1685 and was in such disarray at the time of the Jacobite invasion in 1745 that it proved easier to raise ad hoc bodies of volunteers. This stimulated the reform of the system in 1757, whereby counties were required to ballot for a quota of their able-bodied manpower between the ages of eighteen and fifty (forty-five from 1762) to undertake three years' service in the 'new' militia. The proportion of balloted men who actually served was small since service could be avoided through widespread exemptions, paying a fine or hiring a substitute. Naturally, however, those least able to avoid service were the poorer elements of society, and there were widespread anti-militia riots in both 1757 and when quotas were significantly increased through raising a 'supplementary' militia in England in 1796 and a new militia in Scotland in 1797.

Militiamen were required to undertake (from 1762) twenty-eight days of continuous training each summer, which further reduced its attraction for those in regular employment, and in wartime the militia was embodied for permanent service although normally it was not supposed to serve overseas. Special legislation enabled mainland militia regiments to serve in Ireland when rebellion broke out there in June 1798. The legislation was initiated by the Marquess of Buckingham, whose own regiment, The Royal Bucks King's Own Militia, was rushed to embark at Liverpool by barge on the Grand Junction Canal, the first British military unit ever conveyed by this revolutionary form of transport. Later, The Royal Bucks also formed part of

16

a provisional battalion that saw service, though no fighting, at Bordeaux in 1814: it had received its 'Royal' and 'King's Own' titles for guarding George III (1760-1820) when the King was bathing at Weymouth in 1794.

Increasingly, militiamen were also recruited directly into the army, again requiring special legislation. Indeed, some of the best-known military memoirs of the Revolutionary and Napoleonic Wars were written by those who had first served in the militia, examples being Private Wheeler, William Surtees and Edward Costello. Militiamen were hastily enlisted into the army during the Hundred Days in 1815 when Napoleon returned to France from his first exile on Elba, and many of the **Scots Guards** at the Battle of Waterloo in June 1815 were supposedly still wearing Surrey militia uniforms.

Militia insurance clubs flourished in wartime as the price of substitutes rose dramatically and the ballot became increasingly unpopular. Thus, the ballot was suspended in 1831 and, when the militia was revived during a French invasion scare in 1852, it was on the basis of voluntary enlistment. Indeed, it was the unpopularity of the ballot which long persuaded politicians that introducing compulsion for the regular army would be tantamount to committing political suicide: hence the regular army was not raised by conscription until the First World War. The militia itself finally disappeared in 1908 although the ability to raise it remained on the statute book until 1953. 'Militiamen' was also a term used to describe those conscripted into the regular army under the provisions of the Military Training Act of April 1939, but they had no connection with the original force.

The Volunteers, Yeomanry and Territorials

The militia was always an institution of the state and, in contrast to it, a wide variety of volunteer forces have also existed at other times or simultaneously with it, such as during the 1650s and 1660s, 1715, 1745 and the American War of Independence. The first specific volunteer legislation dates from 1782. However, it was the French Revolutionary and Napoleonic Wars that marked the real flourishing of the volunteer movement with the creation of volunteer infantry and artillery units and mounted volunteer units known as yeomanry. Many of the infantry and artillery volunteer units transferred to a new semi-balloted force known as the local

Officers and men of the 32nd Middlesex (Volunteer Guards) Rifle Volunteer Corps, October 1860. Formed in Marylebone in February 1860, the 32nd was attached to the 11th Middlesex (St George's) RVC in 1863 but was disbanded in 1868.

17

A shapka of the South Bucks Yeomanry Cavalry, 1869. Popularly known as the 'Taplow Lancers', this small independent yeomanry troop existed only from 1838 to 1871 and appears to have worn lancer uniform only in the last two or three years of its existence.

militia in 1808; this was suspended in 1816, although the local militia legislation remained on the statute book until 1921. A few volunteer corps survived post-war reduction but had all vanished by the 1840s, only for the movement to be revived in another French invasion scare in 1859, when most new units were raised as rifle volunteers with a sprinkling of artillery, engineer and mounted units. The yeomanry, meanwhile, survived the post-1815 reductions largely intact and continued to exist throughout the nineteenth century. Curiously, while a new Volunteer Act in 1863 replaced the Volunteer Consolidation Act of 1804 as the legislation governing the rifle volunteers, the yeomanry continued to be governed by the 1804 legislation until 1901. At this point the force was renamed Imperial Yeomanry, a term already used for those units specially raised to serve in the South African War (1899-1902). An infantry unit, The City Imperial Volunteers, was also raised for South Africa while the volunteer force as a whole furnished special service companies to be attached to regular battalions.

Initially, in both the 1790s and, in the case of the volunteers, the 1860s, volunteer and yeomanry units were self-supporting and at liberty both to adopt their own rules and regulations and even to elect their own officers, although appointments were strictly the province of Lords Lieutenant. In Edinburgh in 1859, when all those aspiring to command one rifle volunteer corps had left the room during an election, the remaining three members elected themselves! Similarly, volunteer units were, at least initially, able to set a geographical limit to their patriotism, the Frampton

Colonel Sir Frederick Leighton, then President of the Royal Academy, being presented with an engraved plate to mark his retirement from command of the 20th Middlesex (Artists' Rifles) Rifle Volunteers in 1883. Originally the 38th Middlesex RVC, the Artists later became 28th (County of London) Battalion, The London Regiment.

Volunteers in Gloucestershire deciding in the 1790s that they would be prepared to serve up to 8 miles from the town in the event of French invasion and the Hitchin Association in Hertfordshire but 3 miles. Drawing upon the professional classes and tradesmen in the case of the volunteers and the landed gentry and farming community in the case of the yeomanry, units were also able to design their own uniforms. These were often fanciful and costly: the Earl of Dudley, for example, was said to have spent at least £4000 a year of his own money on The Worcestershire Yeomanry between 1854 and 1871. The involvement of the middle classes in military affairs was also significant when few would otherwise have become so involved. In both the 1790s and the 1860s, for example, there were volunteer units raised by the Inns of Court, that in the 1790s being The Law Association Volunteers and in the 1860s the 23rd (later 14th) Middlesex Rifle Volunteer Corps, which became the Inns of Court Officers Training Corps in 1908. The 21st (later 12th) Middlesex were The Civil Service Rifles, and the 38th (later 20th) Middlesex were The Artists Rifles, which became the 28th (County of London) Battalion, The London Regiment in 1908. With headquarters at Burlington House, the Artists included such distinguished painters as Burne-Jones, Rossetti, Millais and Leighton.

The volunteers and yeomanry were much more significant in terms of local society and community than was the regular army. While the army remained small and mostly overseas, the auxiliaries were by far the more visible representatives of military values. This was especially true of the spectacle provided by the great volunteer

The Artists' Rifles at Victoria railway station, London, awaiting transportation to the Easter Review at Brighton in April 1881. Not always entirely of practical military utility, the reviews were generally superseded by annual camps.

reviews of the 1860s at a time when large gatherings of regular units were simply not seen in England between the camp at Chobham in 1853 and the revival of the annual manoeuvres in 1898, the latter having being briefly initiated between 1871 and 1873. Since the yeomanry was largely maintained after 1815 as an additional constabulary for the support of the civil power, this visibility did not make the force universally popular. Indeed, The Royal Wiltshire Yeomanry received its 'Royal' title in 1831 for its role in suppressing the agricultural disturbances known as the Swing Riots. Similarly, The Manchester and Salford Yeomanry Cavalry, as well as the 15th Hussars, was involved in what became known as the 'Peterloo' massacre in Manchester in August 1819 when there were eleven deaths, although it should be noted that deaths at the hands of the forces of order were comparatively rare in Britain in the years of social, economic and political unrest between 1815 and 1848.

Many regulars continued to believe that the auxiliaries were of little military value, and their training commitment was relatively small, amounting to twenty-four days a year under the Volunteer Consolidation Act of 1804 for those volunteer and yeomanry units wishing to qualify

THE SITE OF St PETERS FIELDS WHERE ON 16th AUGUST 1819 HENRY HUNT RADICAL ORATOR ADDRESSED AN ASSEMBLY OF ABOUT 60000 PEOPLE THEIR SUBSEQUENT DISPERSAL BY THE MILITARY IS REMEMBERED AS 'PETERLOO'

The commemorative plaque at the site of St Peter's Fields in Manchester, scene of the 'Peterloo massacre' by the Manchester and Salford Yeomanry Cavalry and the 15th Hussars.

Field Marshal Lord Kitchener. Appointed Secretary of State for War in August 1914, Kitchener had little time for the 'amateur' soldiers of the Territorial Force.

for government grant towards costs and exemption from the militia ballot, although it also conferred the right to resign upon fourteen days' notice. After 1815, though still covered by the 1804 legislation, the yeomanry were required to undertake eight days' training a year while, after 1863, the volunteers were required to attend nine drills and an annual inspection to qualify for grant. However, training requirements were progressively increased, and in 1901 annual summer camps, which had become a feature of the volunteer movement, were made compulsory. As with the militia, volunteers and yeomanry could not serve overseas without special legislation, but a detachment of the 24th Middlesex (Post Office) Rifle Volunteer Corps served in Egypt in 1882 and received the rare battle honour of 'Egypt 1882', and men of the lst Newcastle and Durham Engineer Volunteers and lst Lancashire Engineer Volunteers also helped construct a military railway at Suakin on the Red Sea coast in 1884. The only other battle honour recorded by auxiliaries before the South African War was that of 'Fishguard', earned by The Castlemartin Yeomanry for service against a small French expedition that landed at Fishguard in Pembrokeshire in February 1797 and surrendered after two days.

Following the South African War, the Haldane reforms in 1908 saw the abolition of the militia and its replacement by the Special Reserve, while the imperial yeomanry and volunteers were combined in a new Territorial Force. It was again the case that Territorials had to accept the so-called imperial service obligation before going overseas during the First World War, and this was a factor in the decision by the Secretary of State for War, Field Marshal Lord Kitchener, to ignore the County Territorial Associations as a means of expanding the wartime army. Instead, Kitchener raised his 'New Armies' as wartime regulars, adding 'service battalions' to regular regiments. These were also volunteers, many being 'Pals Battalions' raised by local communities such as the lst Bradford Pals (16th West Yorkshire Regiment), the Hull Commercials (10th East Yorkshire Regiment), the Public Schools Battalion (16th Middlesex Regiment) and the Glasgow Corporation Tramways Battalion (15th Highland Light Infantry). As a result, individual regiments raised many battalions, The Loyal North Lancashire Regiment, for example, having twenty-one battalions of one kind or another during the war and The Durham Light Infantry having thirty-seven battalions.

However, the Territorial Force still expanded, with twenty-three of its twenty-eight infantry divisions and two of its five mounted (yeomanry) divisions serving overseas. Territorial units suffered over 577,000 casualties. The first Territorial units

Men of the Royal Northumberland Fusiliers after the capture of the St Eloi craters in the Ypres salient in March 1916. Originally the 5th Foot, the regiment raised fifty-two battalions in the First World War and suffered more casualties than any other infantry regiment.

in France were the 1/14th (County of London) Battalion (London Scottish) and the 1/1st Queen's Own Oxfordshire Hussars, the former taking part in a celebrated attack at Messines during the First Battle of Ypres in November 1914. The first of seventy-one Territorial Victoria Crosses was won on Hill 60 in 1915 by Second Lieutenant G. H. Woolley of the 9th (County of London) Battalion (Queen Victoria's Rifles), formerly the 1st Middlesex Rifle Volunteer Corps and direct descendants of The Duke of Cumberland's Sharpshooters of 1794.

In 1920 the Territorial Force was reconstituted as the Territorial Army and made generally liable for overseas service although the liability was hedged with qualifications and not finally resolved until the creation of a single national army in 1939. While being fully integrated within the national wartime army, nine Territorial divisions fought in the 1940 campaign in France and Belgium, one in Norway, four in North Africa, two in Sicily, one in Burma, one at Singapore and eight in the 1944-5 North-west Europe campaign. Territorials won a further seventeen Victoria Crosses. Reconstituted once more in 1947, the post-war Territorials consisted of both volunteers and, until 1966, national servicemen completing their liability. However, the Territorial Army was ruthlessly reduced in 1967, becoming part of the Territorial Army and Volunteer Reserve, the title of Territorial Army being restored in 1982 but the force continuing to suffer reductions. The yeomanry, for example, still comprised twenty-six regiments within the **Royal Armoured Corps** (TA) and twenty-four regiments within the **Royal Regiment of Artillery** (TA) in 1947, but by 1994 there were just thirty-nine sub-units within the RAC, RA, **Royal Engineers**, **Royal Corps of Signals**, **Royal Logistic Corps** and the infantry. The Sussex Yeomanry, for example, had become a field squadron of the **Royal Engineers** TA while the light reconnaissance unit within the RAC known as **The Royal Mercian and Lancastrian Yeomanry** actually carries the traditions of The Duke of Lancaster's Own Yeomanry, The Shropshire Yeomanry, The Staffordshire Yeomanry (Queen's Own Royal Regiment), The Warwickshire Yeomanry and The Queen's Own Worcestershire Hussars.

Wartime expedients

During the French Revolutionary and Napoleonic Wars a number of temporary expedients were utilised to increase Britain's defensive capabilities. These included a so-called Provisional Cavalry in 1796 and plans for a wider *levée en masse* in 1797-8 utilising the powers of a county's High Sheriff to call out the civil power or *posse comitatus*. Under the 1798 Defence of the Realm Act, inhabitants, livestock and vehicles were all registered, and the principle was revived in the Defence Acts of June and July 1803. A Training Act in 1806, which was never implemented but remained on the statute book until 1875, suggested an even wider measure of national military training while two expedients to draft men into the army for home service only were the Army of Reserve (also known as the Additional Army of England) in 1803 and the Permanent Additional Force of 1804-6. It should also be noted that Fencibles – mostly Scottish – raised during the American War of Independence and the Revolutionary and Napoleonic Wars were also regulars raised for home defence only.

The concept of raising additional home defence volunteers was also revived during the two world wars. The Territorial legislation of 1907 had not removed older volunteer legislation from the statute book, and thus in 1914, when it was feared the Germans might invade East Anglia, the Volunteer Training Corps, later renamed the Volunteer Force, was raised from those too old for military service or in reserved occupations. Lacking uniforms at first, the VTC wore 'GR' armbands, drawing the epithets 'Genuine Relics' or 'Grandpapa's Regiment', rather as the Territorials had been 'Saturday Night Soldiers' and earlier volunteers had been caricatured by Gillray in the 1790s and by *Punch* in the 1860s. There were, however, sixteen wartime casualties for the VTC, a party of the 1st Dublin Battalion being unfortunate enough to run into insurgent fire on its way back to Dublin from drill at the start of the Easter Rising in April 1916.

On 14th May 1940 new fears of German invasion resulted in the formation of the Local Defence Volunteers, later to be renamed the Home Guard on 23rd July. Unlike most auxiliaries serving only in Britain, the Home Guard suffered 1206 wartime deaths, some from accidents but most from German aerial attack. Much has been made by historians of the Home Guard of the so-called 'Housemaid's Clause', by which a member could resign on fourteen days' notice until February 1942, but this had been first enshrined in the Volunteer Consolidation Act of 1804, and the Home Guard well illustrates the continuity of the amateur military tradition. Indeed, it was even briefly revived in cadre form between 1952 and 1957.

Territorials from The London Regiment in the Lord Mayor's Parade, 1998. The regiment was formed in 1993 as the infantry battalion for the whole of London.

3. Household Cavalry and Foot Guards

The Household Cavalry and the Guards Division have retained their distinction as the Sovereign's personal regiments. The Household Cavalry always ranked above the cavalry of the line and the Foot Guards above the infantry of the line. Indeed, where officers of the Household Cavalry or Foot Guards served with other regulars of equal rank in the past, they took command. There was also double rank in the Foot Guards until 1872, by which some of their officers were considered to hold a substantive rank in the army at a higher grade than that of their regimental rank. Thus, Foot Guards captains ranked as lieutenant colonels in the army.

As indicated previously, the original mounted and foot regiments of the Restoration period were a merger of the Parliamentarians and exiled Royalists, **The Life Guards** and the **Grenadier Guards** being the latter and the Royal Horse Guards and **Coldstream Guards** the former. Indeed, the Royal Horse Guards, although much favoured by George III, who presented them with silver kettle drums in 1805, were not formally given Household status until 1820 as the Royal Regiment of Horse Guards (The Blues). The additional epithet of The Blues originally derived from the colour of their uniforms in 1661, when they were commanded by the Earl of Oxford and known as The Oxford Blues to distinguish them from a similarly clothed regiment of Dutch Horse Guards that had accompanied William III to England. 'Oxford' was dropped in due course, but 'The Blues' remained in common usage and has been preserved with the present amalgamation of **The Blues and Royals**. Ironically, it was **The Life Guards** that were originally designated Horse Guards and Horse Grenadier Guards until 1788. Horse grenadiers were so named because, instead of carrying swords, they were armed with fusils (a type of early carbine, from the French *fucile*, meaning 'flint') and bayonets.

The Life Guards and **The Blues and Royals** are instantly familiar from their role on state occasions as escorts to the Sovereign and, perhaps most of all, for mounting guard daily at Horse Guards in Whitehall, the site of the War Office from 1722 to 1858 and of the headquarters of the army's Commander-in-Chief until 1871. Both regiments originally wore cuirasses or breast and back plates typical of cavalrymen of the English Civil War, but their use died out in the early eighteenth century and they were reintroduced to the Household Cavalry for the coronation of George IV (1820-30) in 1821. The plumed helmet is of the 1842 dragoon pattern while the white breeches and leather boots are typical of heavy cavalry of the French Revolutionary and Napoleonic Wars. Apart from the

A sentry of the Life Guards mounting guard outside the old Horse Guards Building in Whitehall, London.

The Life Guards, part of the Household Brigade, charging at Waterloo on 18th June 1815.

distinctive dress, the Household Cavalry is also differentiated from other regiments in retaining the rank of Corporal of Horse – once common to all cavalry – instead of sergeant. Similarly, there is a Regimental Corporal-Major instead of a regimental sergeant-major while Drill Sergeant is a rank unique to the Foot Guards.

The Household Cavalry is well known to most members of the public, and even more so are the Foot Guards and their bearskins. Grenadiers – picked soldiers who were originally trained to throw a grenade or bomb, from the Spanish *granada* or

The band of the Coldstream Guards at the Changing of the Guard Ceremony at Buckingham Palace.

The buttons worn in threes on the tunic and the thistle collar badge denote a sentry of the Scots Guards on duty at the Tower of London.

pomegranate – had been introduced into all foot regiments in 1678. The broad-brimmed tricorn hat then worn by most infantry would have impeded the risky operation of throwing the grenade, and therefore they adopted a brimless mitre or fur cap. This fell out of use during the early years of the French Revolutionary and Napoleonic Wars, when English infantry adopted the shako. However, the 1st Foot Guards performed so well against the French Imperial Guard, who had retained the bearskin cap, in the final phase of the Battle of Waterloo on 18th June 1815 that on 29th July the Prince Regent directed that the regiment would now be known as the lst (or Grenadier) Regiment of Foot Guards and adopt the French-style bearskin. Only the grenadier company of the **Coldstream Guards** initially wore the bearskin but they, too, were all directed to wear it by William IV in 1832. It was also William IV who had the 3rd Foot Guards re-designated as the Scots Fusilier Guards in 1831, Queen Victoria assenting to the re-adoption of the older name of **Scots Guards** in 1877. The **Irish Guards** were raised by the Queen's command in April 1900 to commemorate the gallantry of Irish regiments in the South African War at a time when many Irish nationalists were agitating against recruitment in Ireland and some were fighting with the Boers. The **Welsh Guards** were then raised in February 1915, embarking for France in August and going into action at Loos in September.

The Foot Guards regiments can be distinguished from each other by the colour of hackle or plume in the bearskin and by the spacing of buttons on their tunics. The Grenadiers have a white hackle worn on the left and single buttons; the Cold-stream a red hackle worn on the right and buttons in pairs; the Scots no hackle and

Guardsmen in the uniform worn during the Crimean War (1854-6) depicted on the Guards Crimea Memorial in Lower Regent Street, London.

buttons in threes; the Irish a blue hackle worn on the right and buttons in fours; and the Welsh a white and green hackle worn on the left and buttons in fives. In deference to national identity, the collar badge of the **Scots Guards** is a thistle, that of the **Irish Guards** a shamrock leaf and that of the **Welsh Guards** a leek. The **Irish Guards** mark St Patrick's Day (17th March) by wearing a sprig of shamrock issued at a special parade.

Although, on increasing occasions, regiments of the line mount guard at Buckingham Palace, it is the Foot Guards who are overwhelmingly associated with the ceremony. Unless the weather is especially bad, the ceremony takes place daily from spring to autumn and on every other day in winter, the new guard marching from Wellington or Chelsea Barracks to arrive in the palace forecourt at approximately 11.30 a.m. When the Sovereign is in residence, the guard carries the Queen's Colour but, on other occasions, the Regimental Colour. It should be noted, however, that, in the Foot Guards, the Queen's Colour is crimson and the Regimental Colour is the Union Flag, which is the reverse of the practice in line regiments. The Foot Guards also perform the nightly Ceremony of the Keys at the Tower of London, mount guard on Windsor Castle and, since the Gordon Riots in 1780, have usually also maintained the nightly guard on the Bank of England, though this is a duty of the London garrison and, on occasions, has been performed by other regiments or corps. Both Household Cavalry and Foot Guards are seen together for the annual Trooping of the Colour for the Sovereign's official birthday, of which more will be said later, held on Horse Guards Parade on a Saturday in June.

4. Cavalry and Armour

In the seventeenth century cavalry was divided into regiments of horse and regiments of dragoons. The function of the latter, armed originally with a 'dragon' or heavy pistol and later with a carbine, rather than with a sword, was to ride into action but to fight on foot. Dragoons were mounted on poorer and cheaper horses and were also paid less than horse. Prior to 1685, the army had only the troops of **The Life Guards**, the Royal Horse Guards, the Tangier Horse (later The Royal Regiment of Dragoons) and The Royal Regiment of Scots Dragoons, raised in 1681 and later The Royal Scots Greys. However, in 1685 six new regiments of horse and two new regiments of dragoons were raised. Subsequently, in 1746, three regiments of horse were converted to dragoons and, to console them for the loss of status, they were designated as dragoon guards. These were the 1st King's Dragoon Guards, The Queen's Dragoon Guards and the 3rd (Prince of Wales's) Dragoon Guards. The Queen's became better known in 1780 as The Queen's Bays, bay horses having been adopted as regimental mounts after the Seven Years War. In 1959 the lst King's and the Bays were amalgamated as **1st The Queen's Dragoon Guards**, part of the **Royal Armoured Corps**.

Four more dragoon regiments were converted to dragoon guards in 1788, the new 6th Dragoon Guards having once reflected the use of the carbine in being designated The King's Regiment of Carabiniers. In 1826 they once more bore the title as the 6th Dragoon Guards (Carabiniers), being eventually amalgamated with the 3rd Dragoon Guards in 1922 as the 3rd Carabiniers (Prince of Wales's Dragoon Guards) and, after 1971, with The Royal Scots Greys (2nd Dragoons) as **The Royal Scots Dragoon**

An officer of the 13th Hussars in full dress before the First World War.

Guards (Carabiniers and Greys) within the **Royal Armoured Corps**. Like the Bays, the Greys were named after the predominant colour of their horses, adopted in imitation of the Dutch Horse Guards by their commanding officer, Viscount Treviot, although they had also originally worn a grey tunic between 1681 and 1687. They were also identified by wearing grenadier caps, awarded after their performance at the Battle of Ramillies in May 1706 during the War of Spanish Succession, when they captured sixteen enemy colours and, with the 6th (Inniskilling) Dragoons, who earned the same distinction, the French *Régiment du Roi*. At Waterloo in June 1815, in a scene famously captured by the Victorian painter Elizabeth, Lady Butler, the Greys charged at the head of the Union Brigade, chanting 'Scotland for ever'. Sergeant Ewart of the Greys captured the Eagle of the French 45th Regiment, a feat commemorated in the adoption of an eagle as the regimental badge and by Ewart's tomb and monument on the Esplanade of Edinburgh Castle. In the same battle, Captain Kennedy Clark of the 1st Royal Dragoons captured the Eagle of the French 105th Regiment, resulting in a similar addition to their badge.

The function of cavalry on the battlefield, as opposed to dragoons, was to deliver the shock blow at the decisive moment. However, by the eighteenth century many European armies were raising light cavalry for reconnaissance and for outflanking movements and pursuit after battle. In 1756 the British followed suit by adding light dragoon troops to heavy cavalry regiments. They were modelled on the hussars in the Prussian and Austrian service, the word being derived from the conscripted Hungarian light cavalry known as *huszar*, which literally meant 'scout' or 'spy' and was a corruption of the Serbian term for a freebooter. The light dragoon troops were sufficiently successful for five light dragoons regiments to be raised in 1759 while, at varying times between 1763 and 1796, other cavalry regiments were converted to the role and in 1793-5 alone no less than thirteen new regiments of light dragoons were raised. None of these thirteen regiments survived beyond 1822, and only three of those raised in 1759 had a continuous existence until 1922. These were the 15th (The King's) Hussars, the 16th (The Queen's) Lancers and the 17th (The Duke of Cambridge's Own) Lancers. Ironically, the 15th won the first light cavalry battle honour at Emsdorff in July 1760 during the Seven Years War by charging the French in classic heavy cavalry mode and capturing sixteen colours and nine guns as well as

Men of the 7th Hussars sharpening their swords in preparation for active service.

most of five French infantry regiments. As it happened, when 'Emsdorff' was granted as a battle honour in 1768 it was the first in the British Army as a whole, those for the four victories of the Duke of Marlborough during the War of Spanish Succession – Blenheim (August 1704), Ramillies (May 1706), Oudenarde (July 1708) and Malplaquet (September 1709) – were not finally awarded until 1882.

The flamboyant hussar dress itself was not adopted until 1803 by the 10th Light Dragoons while the 15th adopted 'Hussar' as a subtitle three years later. The 8th, 11th and 18th did so subsequently. However, the 3rd, 4th, 7th, 10th, 13th and 14th Light Dragoons only changed their titles to Hussars in 1861. The 3rd, 4th, 7th and 8th are now part of **The Queen's Royal Hussars (The Queen's Own and Royal Irish)** while the 10th, 11th and 14th form part of **The King's Royal Hussars**, and the 13th, 15th and 18th form part of **The Light Dragoons**: all three modern regiments are within the **Royal Armoured Corps**. Two later additions to the hussars were the 19th and 20th, the 1st and 2nd Bengal European Light Cavalry being brought on to the establishment after the disappearance of the East India Company following the Indian Mutiny.

Just as the Hungarian influence was felt among the hussars, so it was Polish influence that shaped the introduction of lancers into the British army, modelled on the Polish lancers that Napoleon had incorporated within his Imperial Guard in 1807. In 1816-17 the 9th, 12th, 16th and 23rd Light Dragoons were converted to the role, adopting the Polish *czapka* or cap and the coloured facing plastron on the tunic. The 19th was converted when the 23rd was disbanded in 1817 and, in turn, the 17th

Light Dragoons were similarly converted in 1821 to replace the disbanded 19th. The 5th was converted in 1861. Some yeomanry regiments also took on the lancer identity, such as the Taplow Troop or South Bucks Yeomanry Cavalry, which had a uniform not unlike that of the 16th Lancers between 1868 and 1871, when this small independent troop disappeared.

The first to use the lance in action were the 16th at Aliwal in January 1846 during the First Sikh War (1845-6) while the 17th Lancers formed part of the Light Brigade with the 8th Hussars, the 11th (Prince Albert's Own) Regiment of (Light) Dragoons (Hussars) and the 4th and 13th Light Dragoons in the Crimean War (1854-6). The brigade was commanded by the notorious Lord Cardigan, who had purchased command of the 11th for a reputed £40,000 in 1836 and spent considerable sums on its uniform. This included the cherry-red trousers, from which the nickname 'Cherry Pickers' or 'Cherrubims' derived, although it has also been claimed that it comes from a detachment caught by the French while picking cherries in an orchard during the Peninsular War (1808-14). As is well known, through a series of misunderstandings, Cardigan mistakenly led the Light Brigade into the North Valley at Balaclava on 25th October 1854: of 673 men who charged, only 193 mounted men returned, with 113 being killed and 134 wounded. The last lancer regiment to be converted, in 1897, was the 21st Hussars, originally the 3rd Bengal European Light Cavalry. Lacking any battle honour, its determination to win one contributed to a reckless charge at Omdurman in the Sudan on 2nd September 1898, in which the regiment lost five officers and sixty-five men killed in less than two minutes when suddenly

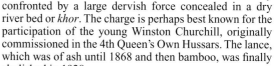

confronted by a large dervish force concealed in a dry river bed or *khor*. The charge is perhaps best known for the participation of the young Winston Churchill, originally commissioned in the 4th Queen's Own Hussars. The lance, which was of ash until 1868 and then bamboo, was finally abolished in 1928.

By the 1920s technological developments had made cavalry largely redundant on a modern battlefield although in the First World War the traditional *arme blanche* role had still proved effective in Palestine and on the Eastern Front. In 1922, therefore, a series of cavalry reductions were effected by amalgamation, creating the so-called 'vulgar fractions' such as the 13th/18th Royal Hussars (Queen Mary's Own) and the 17th/21st Lancers. Normally, the senior numbered regiment took precedence, with the exception of the 16th/5th The Queen's Royal Lancers, which reflected the fact that the 5th (or Royal Irish) Regiment of Dragoons had been disbanded in 1799 and not reformed until 1858, supposedly for recruiting too many former Irish rebels into their ranks following the Irish rebellion of 1798. In 1928 two of the regiments that had survived amalgamation – the 11th Hussars and 12th Lancers – were chosen for mechanisation and re-equipped with armoured cars, with the 11th being the first regular cavalry regiment to lose its horses in April 1928, many yeomanry regiments having already been converted to field artillery or armoured cars. In 1937 the remaining cavalry regiments were converted to tanks and two years later, in April 1939, the **Royal Armoured Corps** came into existence as an umbrella organisation for all armoured units,

An artist's depiction of the disastrous charge of the Light Brigade at Balaclava on 25th October 1854. Both the 8th and the 11th Hussars participated.

Right: *A return of horses of the 4th Light Dragoons found unfit for service in April 1856. Part of the famous Light Brigade, the regiment was still in the Crimea.*

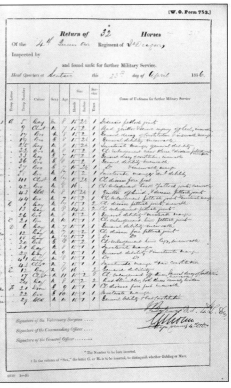

Left: *Presumably intended to depict Balaclava, a dramatic image of the 17th Lancers.*

The second prototype tank, called 'Big Willie' after Kaiser Wilhelm II of Germany, underwent field trials at Hatfield House, Hertfordshire, in January and February 1916. It is seen here on display at Hatfield in 1967.

which role it still performs. It has been argued that this was a belated recognition of the need to develop a coherent armoured doctrine, which could have been better advanced by expanding the Royal Tank Corps.

The Tank Corps itself had been formed on 28th July 1917 from the Heavy Branch, Machine Gun Corps, itself another reflection of the changing battlefield environment. The idea of using pre-war tracked agricultural tractors as the basis for a weapon capable of crossing No Man's Land on the deadlocked Western Front had occurred to a number of individuals at about the same time in the autumn of 1914, although it is Lieutenant Colonel (later Major-General Sir) Ernest Swinton who is usually credited. The tank made its battlefield debut at Flers-Courcelette on the Somme on 15th September 1916 but it was chronically unreliable during the First World War and by no means the breakthrough weapon sometimes portrayed, although it certainly assisted partial breakthroughs at Cambrai on 20th November 1917 and Amiens on 8th August 1918. Apart from their mode of fighting, the Tank Corps was also marked by the adoption in 1925 of the beret, modelled on that worn by the French *Tirailleurs Alpins,* as suitable headgear for use in tanks. The designation 'Royal' was added in October 1923 in recognition of wartime service, the corps being renamed **The Royal Tank Regiment** in April 1939 at the time of its inclusion within the **Royal Armoured Corps**. Once numbering eight, there are currently two battalions within the regiment though, confusingly, they are referred to as regiments rather than as battalions.

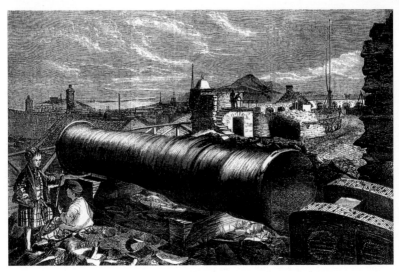

A Victorian engraving of Mons Meg, the fifteenth-century bombard at Edinburgh Castle.

5. Guns and Gunners

Two companies of artillery were formed at Woolwich in May 1716 and, when merged with similar companies at Gibraltar and Minorca in 1722, thereby constituted **The Royal Regiment of Artillery**. Artillery, however, had been a feature of European warfare since the fourteenth century. The enormous bombard at Edinburgh Castle known as Mons Meg dates from the mid fifteenth century. Indeed, the Ordnance Office appears to have been established at the Tower of London between 1414 and 1430. Henry VIII significantly increased the size of his artillery train by purchasing the 'twelve apostles' from the foundries at Malines near Antwerp as well as over a hundred other cannon. He also encouraged a domestic gun-founding industry while his new coastal defence works such as the castles built at Deal and Walmer in Kent displayed contemporary understanding of the science of gunnery to the highest degree. By the time of the Spanish threat in the late sixteenth century, England was capable of producing the best iron ordnance in Europe from the foundries of Kent and Sussex.

Before 1716, however, artillery was a civilian business with gunners in garrisons and in the field hired as needs dictated, although a small nucleus of 'fee'd' gunners was established at the Tower of London in 1486. Even after the establishment of the Royal Artillery, civilian contractors provided the horses and drivers for the artillery train until 1794. The Ordnance Office was placed permanently under a Master General of the Ordnance in 1683. Normally the Master General was a prominent soldier and often doubled as Commander-in-Chief, as, for example, did the Duke of Marlborough and, briefly, the Duke of Wellington. Until 1828 the Master General also sat in the Cabinet. The post was discontinued in 1855 when the civil administration was vested in the Secretary of State for War and the military command of ordnance personnel in the Commander-in-Chief. However, the title of Master General of the Ordnance was revived as a military appointment in 1904.

The Royal Artillery carries no colours since the guns themselves are deemed the equivalent; hence there were many famous episodes when attempts were made to save the guns, as at Maiwand in July 1880 during the Second Afghan War and at Colenso in December 1899 during the South African War. Two Victoria Crosses were won in the attempt at Maiwand and four at Colenso, including a posthumous award to Lieutenant

A large mortar discovered at the Indian fortress of Kurnool in 1839 and now displayed at the Royal Military Academy, Sandhurst.

Freddy Roberts, only son of Field Marshal Lord Roberts. Equally, the regiment had no battle honours as such, adopting the mottoes *Ubique* ('Everywhere') and *Quo Fas et Gloria Ducunt* ('Whither Right and Glory Lead'). However, in 1925 the regiment instituted honour titles for individual batteries to commemorate particular incidents or commanders. The 12th Anti-Tank Battery and 32nd Coast Battery, for example, bore the title of 'Minden', recollecting the battle in August 1759 during the Seven Years War in which the guns were brought into action at the gallop. Similarly, a number of batteries bore the title of 'Gibraltar, 1779-83' to commemorate the service of the artillery during the Spanish siege of the Rock, when, among other feats, red-hot shot was used to destroy enemy floating batteries and Lieutenant George Koehler developed a special 'depression carriage' in 1782 to enable the guns to be fired downwards from positions high on the Rock. Actions throughout the world were recognised: Plassey (1757), Quebec (1759), Talavera (1809), Java (1811), Kirkee (1817), Kabul (1842), Tientsin (1900) and so on. The 171st Field Battery was 'The Broken Wheel' Battery, deriving its title from an incident at the battle of Tel-el-Kebir during the occupation of Egypt in September 1882, when the leading gun lost a wheel in the process of being taken forward against the Egyptian trenches.

A famous depiction by the Victorian battle artist Richard Caton Woodville of the successful attempt to save the guns of E/B Battery of the Royal Horse Artillery during the British defeat at Maiwand in Afghanistan on 27th July 1880.

An engraving commemorating an incident during the defence of Gibraltar by Sir George Eliott when British artillery using red-hot shot destroyed Spanish floating batteries on 13th and 14th September 1782.

The Royal Artillery was formally divided into the Royal Field Artillery and the Royal Garrison Artillery between 1899 and 1924. However, there was also the Royal Horse Artillery formed by the Duke of Richmond when Master General in 1793 to provide more mobile firepower. Armed with six-pounders, the Horse Artillery served extensively in the French Revolutionary and Napoleonic Wars. The Chestnut Troop

The surviving members of 'L'Battery, Royal Horse Artillery working the last remaining 13-pounder at Néry on 1st September 1914. The gun is now in the Imperial War Museum.

The King's Troop, Royal Horse Artillery, firing a salute in London's Green Park.

of Captain Hew Ross, for example, served with the Light Division while two other noted horse artillery troop commanders were Norman Ramsay, who distinguished himself at Fuentes d'Oñoro in May 1811 by galloping his guns to safety through a mass of French cavalry, and Captain Cavalié Mercer, whose journal of the Waterloo campaign is one of the great classics of military memoir. At Néry on 1st September 1914 three Victoria Crosses were won by members of 'L' Battery, RHA, for their gallantry in supporting the 1st Cavalry Brigade against the German 4th Cavalry Division. Under intense fire from twelve German guns, 'L' Battery managed to bring three guns into action, of which two were almost immediately knocked out. After almost three hours, the last two men, both wounded, fired their last round just as reinforcements arrived. A battered 13-pounder from Néry is now displayed in the Imperial War Museum. The 13-pounder is the gun used by the sole remaining mounted troop, **The King's Troop, Royal Horse Artillery**, which is seen on ceremonial occasions such as firing the salute on the Sovereign's birthday in Hyde Park, and also familiar from its spectacular 'musical ride' with guns and limbers at the Royal Tournament. The Troop was formed in 1946 and, by permission of Queen Elizabeth II, retains the title of King's Troop in memory of her father, George VI (1936-52). It took part in Trooping of the Colour for the Queen's Birthday Parade for the first time in 1998.

Together with engineers, gunners were generally more professional than infantrymen or cavalrymen in earlier centuries because of the technical demands of their arm of service. It is not surprising, therefore, that it was the Royal Artillery who first experimented with the rockets developed by Sir William Congreve in 1800. In June 1813 a rocket detachment took part in the Battle of Leipzig as part of the Allied army while one of the two RHA rocket troops was at Waterloo. However, the weapon proved somewhat unreliable, and so too was Hale's rocket, which superseded that of Congreve in 1867. In the First World War development in artillery techniques such as sound ranging and flash spotting was considerable, contributing greatly to the improvement of British tactical methods by 1917-18.

6. Infantry of the Line

At least until the First World War, cavalry, artillery and the other arms were there, for all intents and purposes, to serve the infantry in the British Army. Indeed, the Emperor Napoleon referred to infantry as the 'lord of the battlefield', and it has usually represented the majority of most armies because it is more flexible than the other arms. The word itself comes from the French derivative of the Italian *fante*, originally a retainer who followed his lord to war much as an esquire followed the knight in the medieval period. One development of the so-called military revolution in the early modern period was the emergence in the sixteenth century of infantry comprising both musketeers and pikemen, as still represented by the Company of Pikemen and Musketeers of **The Honourable Artillery Company**. However, as firearms improved, so by about 1700 the number of pikemen declined, the more reliable flintlock having superseded the matchlock. The last nail in the coffin of the pikeman was the adoption of the bayonet: the first early plug bayonets appeared in France in 1647 but were replaced by the socket bayonet, enabling infantrymen to continue to fire, by the end of the seventeenth century. Indeed, at the Battle of Killiecrankie in 1689 English troops, still equipped with plug bayonets and unable to reload, were put to flight by a Highland charge. The Scottish victor in the cause of James II, James Graham of Claverhouse, who was killed in the battle, is remembered in song as 'Bonnie Dundee'. The experience speeded the adoption of the socket bayonet, and all English infantry possessed flintlocks and socket bayonets by 1703.

It was under Marlborough during the War of Spanish Succession that British infantry began to earn a particular reputation for its musketry. A British battalion was divided into eighteen or twenty-four platoons in three ranks with the front rank kneeling. Firing was by groups of platoons, with one third of the battalion always ready to fire, and a continuous discharge of fire was kept up. By contrast, the French company firing system was not as effective, and British volleys proved devastating as at Fontenoy in May 1745 when over 700 Frenchmen were hit in the opening exchange. As explained previously, grenadier companies were added to battalions in

Musketeers of the Honourable Artillery Company at the Lord Mayor's Show in 1998.

The 61st Foot, later the 2nd Battalion, The Gloucestershire Regiment, during the capture of Guadeloupe in the French West Indies in 1759. The island was captured by the British again in 1794, 1810 and 1815 but was finally restored to France in 1816.

1678 although the use of the grenade had ceased by 1714. They had been the first to be armed with a shorter flintlock carbine or *fusil*, followed by those designated as artillery escorts since the lighted matches necessary for matchlocks were dangerous in the extreme when used close to gunpowder. Thus the 7th Foot, raised in June 1685 from two companies of guards at the Tower of London, where the army's ordnance was stored, was known as The Ordnance Regiment or Royal Regiment of Fuziliers. It lost the title in 1782 when, under the first attempt to link regiments to counties, it found itself allocated to Derbyshire. However, the original link with the Tower was restored in 1881 with re-designation as The Royal Fusiliers (City of London) Regiment. While The Royal Scots Fusiliers, now part of **The Royal Highland Fusiliers, 2nd Battalion The Royal Regiment of Scotland**, also came on to the English establishment from Scotland as artillery guards in 1688, other regiments were later designated as fusiliers primarily as a mark of honour.

The two original fusilier regiments and the later creations – The Royal Northumberland Fusiliers, The Lancashire Fusiliers, The Royal Inniskilling Fusiliers, The Royal Irish Fusiliers and The Royal Welch Fusiliers (the title was 'Welsh' prior to 1921) – all maintained the tradition of the original connection with grenadiers by wearing the cut-down version of the grenadier fur cap, adopting a bursting grenade as their cap badge and usually including 'The British Grenadiers' among their regimental marches. The two Irish regiments disappeared in 1922, and The Royal Fusiliers and The Lancashire, The Royal Northumberland and The Royal Warwickshire Fusiliers (so designated only in 1963) have all been subsumed in **The Royal Regiment of Fusiliers**. Created as a four-battalion regiment in 1968, it was reduced to three in 1969 and to two battalions in

The Royal Welch Fusiliers in 1808, showing the cut-down version of the grenadier fur cap adopted by fusilier regiments.

39

The 46th Foot, later the Duke of Cornwall's Light Infantry, in action at Brandywine, Pennsylvania, in September 1777. So that the Americans, who vowed revenge, should not mistake them, the 46th and 49th both adopted red hat feathers after the action.

1992, the third battalion serving in the Gulf War as part of 4th Armoured Brigade.

Just as grenadier companies were added to infantry battalions in the seventeenth century, so light companies were added between 1758 and 1763 and, again, after 1770, both in imitation of developments already occurring in European armies and under the influence of irregular warfare in North America, where both British and French learned the value of the woodcraft practised by Indians and colonists alike. On the Monongahela near Fort Duquesne in July 1755, for example, a force of British and colonial troops under the hapless Major-General Edward Braddock found volleys no answer to French-led Indians firing on the column from concealment on all sides. Subsequently, grenadier and light companies were frequently detached from battalions for collective shock action. At Brandywine in September 1777, during the American War of Independence, the light companies of the 46th and 49th Foot (later part of The Duke of Cornwall's Light Infantry and The Royal Berkshire Regiment and now respectively within the 5th and 1st Battalions, **The Rifles**) while acting on such detached service scored a notable success against an American force. The Americans vowed revenge, and the two companies defiantly dyed their hat feathers red so that the Americans should not mistake them if they met again. Thereafter, in memory of the incident, the DCLI wore two red feathers in their foreign service helmets while the Royal Berkshires adopted a red cloth patch worn behind their cap badge. American service also persuaded the British to adopt a two-rank firing line rather than a three-rank line.

The continuing process of reduction since the end of the Second World War has resulted in the loss of many old infantry regiments. However, this is not a new process because the army was regularly reduced after earlier wars. Of sixty-nine new regiments raised after 1702, for example, only thirty-four were still in existence by 1712 as British participation in the War of Spanish Succession came to an end. Since 1945 some regiments have chosen to disband rather than be amalgamated, such as The Cameronians (Scottish Rifles) and The York and Lancaster Regiment in 1968. The last three surviving English county regiments to remain unscathed were swept away in 2006 and 2007.

7. Light Infantry and Rifles

Alongside the formation of the light infantry companies in North America during the Seven Years War, it was decided to create whole battalions of light infantry, the first in 1755 being the four-battalion 62nd (Royal American) Regiment, renumbered as the 60th in 1757 and later The King's Royal Rifle Corps. Four years later the 85th (Royal Volunteers) Light Infantry were raised in Shrewsbury although they were then disbanded in 1763 and the number re-allocated to a new creation in 1779. Commanded by Henry Bouquet, a Swiss soldier of fortune, the Royal Americans were mostly Swiss and German. They were trained to act on their own initiative and clothed in green uniforms; the better marksmen were also armed with rifles although it was not until 1797 that a fifth battalion of the 60th was entirely equipped with rifles. That reflected the lessons of the early campaigns of the French Revolutionary and Napoleonic Wars.

The conscripted citizen armies of the French Republic, who lacked a more formal military training in the rigid movements of the eighteenth-century battlefield, covered their advancing mass columns with swarms of skirmishers. The Duke of York, who had commanded the British expeditionary force in the unsuccessful campaign in the Netherlands in 1793-4, believed the French could only be matched by equally flexible British skirmishers. As a result, a number of battalions were converted to the light infantry role, the fifth battalion being added to the 60th under the command of the Austrian-born Lieutenant Colonel Baron Francis de Rottenburg. In 1800 an experimental rifle corps of specially selected men, armed with the new Baker rifle, was raised by Colonel Coote Manningham and Lieutenant Colonel William Stewart. Renamed in 1802 as the 95th Foot, it was later The Rifle Brigade. In 1803 it was decided to go further, and a corps of light infantry – the nucleus of the later Light Division – was formed at Shorncliffe Camp in Kent under the direction of Major-General Sir John Moore. Like the 60th, the 95th were uniformed in green, but the two line battalions sent to Shorncliffe – the 43rd and 52nd – remained in red, becoming linked in 1881 as The Oxfordshire Light Infantry. Under the command of Major-General Robert 'Black Bob' Craufurd, a strict disciplinarian, The Light Division proved its worth in acting as rearguard during the retreat of the British army landed in Spain under Moore's command to Corunna and Vigo between December 1808 and January 1809. Later in July 1809 the 43rd covered 52 miles (84 km) in just twenty-six hours trying to reach Talavera in time to fight with Wellington's army.

The other regiments converted to a light infantry role between 1808 and 1809 were the 51st (later 1st Battalion, The King's Own Yorkshire Light Infantry), the 68th (later 1st Battalion, The Durham Light Infantry) and the 85th (later 2nd Battalion, The King's Shropshire Light Infantry). The 13th (later The Somerset Light Infantry) was converted in 1822 and the 32nd (later 1st Battalion, The Duke of Cornwall's Light Infantry) received the title in 1858 for its service in defence of Lucknow during the Indian Mutiny. All these light infantry regiments, together with The King's Royal Rifle Corps, The Rifle Brigade and The Oxford and Bucks Light Infantry, are subsumed within **The Rifles**.

Both light infantry and rifle regiments marched at 140 paces to the minute with rifles at the trail and had bugle bands and bugles as cap badges. Movements were also regulated by bugle rather than drum. They also fixed 'swords' rather than bayonets. The two rifle regiments – the 60th and 95th – were further distinguished, by black

The characteristic bugle badge of the Light Infantry, signifying the tradition of movements regulated by bugle rather than drum.

buttons and equipment and by not carrying colours, with the result that battle honours are carried on the silver crests of officers' pouch belts and on the drums.

The rifle tradition may also be found in **The 1st Royal Gurkha Regiment** and **The 2nd Royal Gurkha Regiment**, who, with the much reduced components of the **Queen's Gurkha Engineers**, **Queen's Gurkha Signals** and **Gurkha Transport Regiment**, are all that remain of the Brigade of Gurkhas. The British first encountered the Gurkhas of the mountainous kingdom of Nepal in the eighteenth century, the name originally deriving from the small town of Gorkha, named after the Hindu saint Gorakhnath. The martial qualities of the Goorkhas, as they were then known to the British, became evident when the East India Company found itself at war with Nepal between 1814 and 1816, and Gurkhas were recruited into the Company's army during a truce in 1815. Following the war, Britain and Nepal concluded a treaty of perpetual friendship and alliance, by which Nepal allowed its subjects to enlist with the Company. During the Indian Mutiny (1857) the Gurkhas remained loyal, and it was during the siege of Delhi

The 2nd Goorkhas (then the Prince of Wales's Own) in Malta in June 1878, an Indian expeditionary force having been despatched to the Mediterranean in case Britain became involved in the Russo-Turkish War. Subsequently the Indian troops occupied Cyprus.

The Gurkha Memorial off Whitehall, London, has a Gurkha wearing the uniform from the First World War.

that the Sirmoor Battalion (later the 2nd King Edward VII's Own Goorkha Rifles) forged a particular link with the 60th Foot (The King's Royal Rifle Corps), from which derived the custom of Gurkhas wearing rifle green. Ultimately there were ten Gurkha regiments of two battalions each in the British Indian Army, still armed with the celebrated *kukri*, although they also developed a liking for bagpipes. Of the varying tribes that inhabited Nepal, the Magars and Gurungs of western and central Nepal were those regarded by the British as the best recruits, and they largely filled seven of the Gurkha regiments while two, the 7th and 10th, took Limbus and Rais from eastern Nepal and one, the 9th, took taller men of Rajput origin from the west. Gurkha exploits have become legendary, and stories about the Gurkhas have approximated to myth as in the apocryphal story of the Gurkha kicked in the head by a mule: while the Gurkha complained of a headache, the mule went lame!

When India became independent in 1947, it was agreed to divide the brigade between India and Britain. Those transferring to the British Army were the 2nd King Edward VII's Own Goorkha Rifles (The Sirmoor Rifles), the 6th Queen Elizabeth's Own Gurkha Rifles, the 7th Duke of Edinburgh's Own Gurkha Rifles and 10th Princess Mary's Own Gurkha Rifles. The 7th served in the Falklands campaign in 1982 as part of 5th Infantry Brigade. In 1994 the 2nd and 6th amalgamated to form **The 1st Royal Gurkha Regiment** while the 7th became **The 2nd Royal Gurkha Regiment** and the 10th became The 3rd Royal Gurkha Regiment. With the withdrawal of Britain from Hong Kong in 1996, The 3rd Royal Gurkha Regiment was disbanded.

Although not a rifle regiment, there is one additional unit that has been considered part of the British Army since 1958 but which is recruited and stationed overseas: **The Gibraltar Regiment**, which originated as the Gibraltar Defence Force in 1939.

43

8. Highland and Lowland

By 1914 the British Army was overwhelmingly English in its composition, but this had not always been the case as the Scots and the Irish had provided large numbers of recruits in the eighteenth and early nineteenth century. Although there was a union of the Scottish and English crowns in 1603 with the accession of James VI of Scotland as James I (1603-25) of England, the army in Scotland remained on a separate establishment until the Act of Union in 1707. Scots also had a long tradition of mercenary service, not least in the Dutch and French armies, the Scottish Archer Guard of France being supposedly established in the thirteenth century. Some Scottish regiments taken on to the English establishment claimed precedence over other regiments by virtue of their previous service overseas. The Royal Scots (The Royal Regiment), for example, was taken on the English establishment in 1662 as the 1st or Scots Regiment of Foot, having been raised as independent companies in the service of Sweden in 1625 by Sir John Hepburn, who had also been in Bohemian service. Technically, The Royal Scots became a British regiment in 1633 when Charles I permitted Hepburn to raise recruits in Scotland for a new regiment to be raised in the service of France. Indeed, their nickname was 'Pontius Pilate's Bodyguard', supposedly arising from a precedence dispute between the then Régiment de Douglas and the French Régiment de Picardie in 1643: the French claimed to have been on duty the night after the Crucifixion while the Scots reputedly claimed that, as Pontius Pilate's Bodyguard, they would not have been asleep if they had been on duty. Reclaimed by Charles II, the regiment was subsequently loaned to France again but was recalled to the British establishment in 1676.

The Scottish Highlands and Lowlands were distinct entities not only geographically – the traditional division between the two ran along the Strathmore valley – but also

The Black Watch advancing on the Russian positions at the Battle of the Alma in the Crimea on 20th September 1854.

A sergeant of the 79th, The Queen's Own Highlanders in the pre-1914 full dress. The 79th was the only single-battalion regiment in the army between 1872 and 1897.

increasingly in terms of social and economic development, Highland society being characterised by the prevalence of the clan system. Various independent Highland companies that were intended to keep order existed in the late seventeenth century, but the shock of the first Jacobite rebellion in 1715 led to their disbandment. However, the concept was revived in 1725 when four new independent companies were formed. Two more were added in 1729 to what was known as *am Freiceadan Dubh* (The Black Watch) and another four in 1739 when the whole was brought on the British establishment as the 42nd (Royal Highland) Regiment of Foot, 1st Battalion, **The Black Watch, 3rd Battalion, the Royal Regiment of Scotland)**. The second Jacobite rebellion in 1745, in which the army of the Young Pretender, Prince Charles Edward Stuart ('Bonnie Prince Charlie'), advanced as far south as Derby, resulted in the disarming of the Highlands and a prohibition of Highland dress, but the Black Watch was permitted to retain bonnet and plaid and the traditional weapons of broadsword and dirk. Moreover, the 42nd or Government Tartan became the basis for most of the other military tartans, which are distinct from clan tartans.

Highland dress was also permitted in regiments subsequently raised in the Highlands, of which there were no less than thirty-seven between 1725 and 1800 in addition to the fencible regiments supposedly raised for home service only during the American War of Independence and the French Revolutionary and Napoleonic Wars. Scottish recruitment served to alleviate the overpopulation of the Highlands but, in so doing, also provided an outlet for Highland and clan identity, albeit mostly overseas,

45

A sentry of the Royal Highland Fusiliers at Edinburgh Castle in 1987. Wearing the distinctive trews of the Lowland infantry, the regiment was created in 1959 from the amalgamation of the Royals Scots Fusiliers and the Highland Light Infantry.

and a realistic measure of security for governments in London concerned at the potential risks of further unrest. Nonetheless, it was not always easy to maintain the numbers of Highland recruits, and in 1809 six regiments lost their Highland status. By the end of the Napoleonic Wars, there were five recognised Highland regiments, recognised in the sense that they wore the kilt or *feileadh beag*, which had developed around 1810, when the original wrap-around plaid belted at the middle was separated into kilt and shoulder plaid. These five were the 42nd, 78th, 79th, 92nd and 93rd. Five regiments also retained some characteristics of Highland origin although not wearing the kilt: the 72nd, 73rd, 74th, 75th and 91st. After 1881 the 42nd and 73rd were linked as The Black Watch (Royal Highland Regiment), the 72nd and 78th as The Seaforth Highlanders (Ross-shire Buffs, The Duke of Albany's), the 75th and 92nd as The Gordon Highlanders, and the 91st and 93rd as The Argyll and Sutherland Highlanders (Princess Louise's), while the 79th was a single battalion regiment, The Queen's Own Cameron Highlanders, until forming a second battalion in 1897. In 1961 the Seaforths and Camerons amalgamated as The Queen's Own Highlanders (Seaforths and Camerons), and in 1994 this regiment was amalgamated with the Gordons as The Highlanders (since 2006 the Highlanders, 4th Battalion The Royal Regiment of Scotland).

Of the regiments of Highland origin only the 74th was excluded from being linked once more with kilted regiments in 1881. Instead, it became the 2nd Battalion, The Highland Light Infantry and was consigned to trews (tartan trousers), which, though originally as much Highland as Lowland garb, came to be associated in 1881 with the latter because it was then that they changed from ordinary line infantry uniform to doublet and trews. However, The Highland Light Infantry did take up the kilt again in 1947; also it was the only light infantry regiment to march at the slope and at only 120 paces to the minute. The Royal Scots and The King's Own Scottish Borderers (both trews regiments) also adopted the blue Kilmarnock bonnet with diced border, red *tourie* and cock's feathers although The Royal Scots Fusiliers wore the fusilier cap and The Cameronians were a rifle regiment.

9. Welsh and Irish

Unlike Scotland and Ireland, there was never a separate military establishment for Wales, but, excluding the **Welsh Guards**, there are regiments particularly associated with the principality, namely The Royal Welch Fusiliers, The Welch Regiment – again spelled 'Welsh' prior to 1921 – and The South Wales Borderers: the latter two were amalgamated in 1969 as The Royal Regiment of Wales (24th/41st Foot). Ironically, the 24th, later The South Wales Borderers, celebrated for their role in the Zulu War, not least in the film *Zulu*, were actually the 2nd Warwickshire Regiment at the time although they had established their depot at Brecon in 1873 under localisation and did recruit among the Welsh communities living astride the border with England. The Royal Welch Fusiliers and The Royal Regiment of Wales (24th/41st Foot) are now part of The Royal Welsh.

The 1/24th had been in South Africa since 1875 and took part in the Ninth Cape Frontier (Kaffir) War in 1877-8 while the 2/24th arrived at the Cape in March 1878 to participate in the latter stages of the same war. On 22nd January 1879 five companies of the 1/24th and one company of the 2/24th died to a man when the Zulus overwhelmed the British camp at Isandlwana. Two subalterns of the 1/24th, Teignmouth Melvill and Nevill Coghill, died carrying the Queen's Colour of the 1/24th along what became known as Fugitive's Trail. On 4th February the colour was recovered from

The colours of the 1/24th Foot (later the South Wales Borderers), recovered from the Mzinyathi (Buffalo) river, being returned to the survivors of the regiment at Helpmakaar in Natal in February 1879.

A fanciful scene of the recovery of the colours of the 24th Foot following the battle of Chillianwallah on 13th January 1849 during the Second Sikh War. No one had noticed the colours wrapped around the body of a private soldier when he was buried.

the Mzinyathi (Buffalo) river and later decorated by Queen Victoria with a wreath of immortelles in July 1880. At the time the Victoria Cross could not be conferred posthumously, but King Edward VII (1901-10) changed the rules in 1907 and Melvill and Coghill were among the first to be recognised retrospectively. Isandlwana was not the first time the 24th had lost its Queen's Colour for at Chillianwallah in January 1849 during the Second Sikh War (1848-9) a private had wrapped it around his body for safe keeping after the ensign carrying it had been killed but he, too, was killed and his body buried without anyone noticing.

Meanwhile, a portion of the victorious Zulu army had swept on from Isandlwana to the mission station of Rorke's Drift, guarded by B Company of 2/24th under Lieutenant Gonville Bromhead with assorted casuals and hospital patients, the whole commanded by Lieutenant John Chard of the **Royal Engineers**. The 152 defenders held off between 3000 and 4000 Zulus for twelve hours over the 22nd and 23rd January. Eleven of them were awarded the Victoria Cross, of whom seven, including Bromhead, were from the 2/24th.

The best-known custom associated with a Welsh regiment is that of 'eating the leek' in The Royal Welch Fusiliers on St David's Day (1st March). All ranks wear leeks in their head-dress, and in each dining hall the latest joined recruit in each company eats a leek brought around

The appropriate badge of the Welsh Guards is the leek, customarily worn in Welsh regiments on St David's Day (1st March).

A memorial window in Wrexham church to The Royal Welsh Fusiliers. It depicts modern and original uniforms in front of the band, and with the regimental mascot.

by the commanding officer accompanied by the drum-major, a drummer, the goat-major and the regimental mascot. In the officers' mess an even more elaborate ritual is followed for the latest-joined officer and all those present, irrespective of rank or unit, who have not previously eaten a leek with the regiment. The custom was also observed in The Royal Regiment of Wales.

Ireland is an island whose history has been very much shaped by conflict, but a military career became acceptable to Irishmen of all political and religious persuasions in the absence of other opportunities. Both Protestant Irish and Gaelic Irish placed a high value on martial virtues, and the Protestant Anglo-Irish virtually colonised the high command of the British army. Among famous Anglo-Irish soldiers may be counted Wellington, Roberts, Wolseley, Kitchener, Alexander and Montgomery. The Protestant community also had an amateur military tradition akin to that on the mainland of Britain from the eighteenth century onwards while the Gaelic Irish enjoyed a mercenary tradition like that of Scotland from the sixteenth century onwards as 'the wild geese'. Both communities have also had something of a paramilitary tradition as evidenced by the rival volunteer movements before the First World War, the Ulster Volunteer Force and the Irish Volunteers. During the war the Ulster Volunteer Force formed the 36th Division of Kitchener's 'New Army' while elements of the Irish Volunteers were to be found in both the 10th and 16th Irish Divisions. Indeed, the title 'Irish Brigade', whether that in the French Army in the eighteenth century, the Union Army during the American Civil War or the British Army's 38th Irish Brigade in the Second World War, had an almost talismanic quality, although the consequence was that Irishmen frequently found themselves confronting each other on battlefields across the globe, as at Malplaquet in September 1709 when the 18th Foot, then known simply as The Royal Regiment of Ireland, directly confronted its equivalent in the French service. The Irish had been a substantial proportion of the army's rank and file from the late eighteenth century until the mid nineteenth century. In 1830, for example, an estimated 42.2 per cent of the rank and file had been Irish but, with greater emigration to North America as a consequence of the famine in the 1840s, this had fallen to just 9.1 per cent by 1913.

The oldest Irish regiment was the 18th Foot, later The Royal Irish Regiment, raised in 1684, followed by the 27th Foot, later the 1st Battalion, The Royal Inniskilling Fusiliers, raised in 1689 from those who had defended Enniskillen against the forces of King James II, James having fled to Ireland when William III landed in England. The 83rd, 86th, 87th and 88th were all raised in 1793, the 83rd and 86th becoming linked in 1881 as The Royal Irish Rifles and the 87th and 89th as The Royal Irish

The 88th Foot, later the 1st Battalion, The Connaught Rangers at the storming of the citadel at Badajoz on 6th April 1812 during the Peninsular War in Spain. The Sherwood Foresters also participated in the assault, and one of its officers hoisted his scarlet coatee in place of the French flag to signify the town had fallen.

Fusiliers. The 88th became the 1st Battalion, The Connaught Rangers, the second battalion being formed from the 94th, which ironically traced its origins to a Scottish regiment in Dutch service. Even more bizarre, in 1881 most of the East India Company's European regiments that were transferred to Crown service after the Indian Mutiny were given Irish titles. Thus the 102nd and 103rd became The Royal Dublin Fusiliers, the 101st and 104th became The Royal Munster Fusiliers, and the 109th was linked with the 100th – originally raised in Canada in 1858 – as The Prince of Wales's Leinster Regiment (Royal Canadians).

With the division of Ireland following the Anglo-Irish War (1919-21), those regiments linked with southern Ireland – the Connaughts, the Munsters, the Leinsters, the Royal Dublin Fusiliers and the Royal Irish Regiment – were disbanded while the Royal Irish Rifles was renamed The Royal Ulster Rifles. In 1968 The North Irish Brigade of The Royal Ulster Rifles, The Royal Inniskilling Fusiliers and The Royal Irish Fusiliers were converted into a new three-battalion regiment, The Royal Irish Rangers. However, partition did not affect the continued recruitment of southern Irishmen into the British Army, The Royal Irish Fusiliers in particular drawing about a fifth of its recruits from the south in the inter-war period, while both The Royal Ulster Rifles and The Royal Inniskilling Fusiliers also recruited across the religious divide in Northern Ireland. Similarly, in 1989 about a fifth of the 2nd Royal Irish Rangers were from the south. The onset of 'the Troubles' in 1969 brought the replacement of the Ulster Special Constabulary with a new part-time regiment, The Ulster Defence Regiment, formed in 1970. In 1992 the UDR and The Royal Irish Rangers were amalgamated in a new regiment, **The Royal Irish Regiment (27th Inniskilling, 83rd, 87th and UDR)**, a title reflecting that of the senior Irish regiment in the old army, the 18th, disbanded in 1922, which had recruited entirely in what had become the Irish Republic.

10. Special Forces

In their way, the raising of grenadier and light infantry companies in the eighteenth century and the subsequent creation of light infantry and rifle regiments reflected the response to special needs identified as warfare developed. The establishment of first the Machine Gun Corps and then the Royal Tank Corps during the First World War were similar responses to changing circumstances. Of course, ad hoc formations were also often created in emergencies. During the Second World War a whole range of special units was created, many of which were intended to undertake operations behind enemy lines. The Chindits, for example, were formed by the controversial and unorthodox Orde Wingate to undertake 'long-range penetration' behind Japanese lines in Burma in 1942, 77th Indian Infantry Brigade being converted for this purpose for the first operation in 1943 and 14th, 16th, 77th, 111th and 3rd West African Brigades being used for the second operation in 1944.

More successful were those smaller units raised in the North African campaign such as Major Ralph Bagnold's Long Range Desert Group and 'L' Detachment of the Special Air Service Brigade, the latter formed in 1941 by David Stirling of the **Scots Guards**. In January 1943 Stirling's much expanded unit became lst Special Air Service Regiment (1 SAS), to which was added 2 SAS, commanded by his brother, William, in April 1943. The two regiments fought in Sicily, Italy and North-west Europe before being disbanded in 1946. However, the concept was revived within the Territorial Army in 1947 with the creation of 21 SAS from the old Artists Rifles. Then, during the Malayan Emergency (1948-60), a new unit called the Malayan Scouts was created under the command of the former Chindit Michael Calvert to take the war to the communist guerrillas operating in the deep jungle. Men from 21 SAS were attached to the Malayan Scouts and in 1952 **22nd Special Air Service Regiment** was formally added to the army's establishment. Its tasks include counter-insurgency, as during the Indonesian/Malaysian 'Confrontation' (1962-6) in Borneo and the Dhofar campaign in Oman between 1970 and 1975; intelligence gathering as in the Falklands War (1982) and the Gulf War (1990); and counter-terrorism, memorably illustrated by its storming of the Iranian embassy in London to end a hostage crisis in May 1980.

Before forming the SAS, Stirling had been serving in a commando group known

as Layforce, and, while commandos are now associated with the **Corps of Royal Marines**, there were both army and marine commando units during the Second World War. His Majesty's Marine Forces were formed in April 1755, but the Corps traces its origins to the Duke of York and Albany's Maritime Regiment of Foot, also known as the Admiral's Regiment, which was partly raised from the London Trained Bands in 1664. Awarded the laurel wreath for

A sculptured Chindit on the war memorial to Wingate's long-range penetration formations behind Japanese lines in Burma during the Second World War. 'Chindit' was derived from the Burmese word for the stone lions characteristically found at the entrances of Buddhist temples.

Two panels from the Royal Marines Memorial in The Mall close to Admiralty Arch. One depicts Marine artillery supporting the attack on Boer positions at Graspan on 25th November 1899 during the South African War; the other shows the defence of the European legations in Peking against the Boxers in 1900.

their role at the siege of Belle Isle in 1761, the Marines received their royal title in 1802, ranking after the 49th Foot in precedence. From 1862 to 1923 the Royal Marine Light Infantry and Royal Marine Artillery existed as separate corps, artillery companies having been introduced in 1804. A number of regiments experienced sea service in the eighteenth century including the 4th Foot, later The King's Own Royal Regiment (Lancaster), and the 7th Foot, later The Royal Fusiliers. The 30th, later 1st Battalion, The East Lancashire Regiment, the 31st Foot, later 1st Battalion, The East Surrey Regiment, and the 32nd Foot, later 1st Battalion, The Duke of Cornwall's Light Infantry, were all originally raised as marines.

The 62nd Foot, later 1st Battalion, The Wiltshire Regiment, was taken on board the fleet of Admiral Boscawen as marines, earning the battle honour 'Louisburg' for its service in July 1758 off this French fortress in Nova Scotia. Similarly, the 69th, later 2nd Battalion, The Welch Regiment, was placed at the Admiralty's disposal as marines in the Seven Years War and continued to serve on board the fleet for much of the remainder of the eighteenth century. For the role of its men on various ships at the Battle of the Saints in April 1782, the 69th was given the right to bear a naval crown with the words '12th April 1782' on its regimental colour, while it also had the battle honour of St Vincent 1797. Naval crowns commemorating the naval battle of the Glorious First of June on 1st June 1794 were also borne on the Colours of The Queen's Royal Regiment (West Surrey) and The Worcestershire Regiment.

Other regiments distinguished themselves at sea without being marines since it was their fate to display heroism in shipwrecks. Perhaps the most celebrated episode is that of the troopship *Birkenhead* off South Africa in January 1852, when the troops on board – mostly young drafts for nine different regiments including the 12th Foot, later 1st Battalion, The Suffolk Regiment – stood fast in their ranks

A detachment of Royal Marines at the Queen Mother's funeral parade, 2002.

while the women and children were taken off in the only three boats that could be launched. The story of the men's heroism – less than half survived – was reputedly ordered to be read to every regiment in the Prussian Army. Five years later, men of the 54th, later 2nd Battalion, The Dorset Regiment, saved the *Sarah Sands* off Mauritius by throwing the powder kegs overboard when the ship caught fire and the seamen had taken to the boats: Sarah Sands Day is still celebrated annually in **The 1st Battalion, the Rifles**. The lst Battalion, The King's Royal Rifle Corps similarly commemorated the loss of the *Warren Hastings* off Mauritius in January 1897, when all on board survived through good discipline, by sounding ship's time in barracks on the original ship's bell.

The Royal Marines are organised into 3rd Commando Brigade, comprising Nos 40, 42 and 45 Commando, and the Commando Logistics Regiment, Royal Marines. The brigade fought in the Falklands in 1982 alongside the 2nd and 3rd Battalions, **The Parachute Regiment**, whose red berets are as familiar as the green berets of the Marines. The Paras date from a direction to the chiefs of staff by Winston Churchill on 22nd June 1940 to form a parachute corps of at least 5000 men in imitation of those in the German and Russian armies. The men originally chosen for parachute training were drawn from No 2 Commando. An Airborne Division was formed by Major-General (later Lieutenant-General) Sir Frederick 'Boy' Browning in October 1941, and the regiment received its first battle honour for the raid on Bruneval in February 1942 when C Company, 2nd Parachute Battalion seized a German *Würzburg* radar set from its installation on the cliffs of the northern coast of France. Later in the war 6th Airborne Division led the assault on Normandy in June 1944 while 1st Airborne Division was committed to the tragic Arnhem operation in September 1944.

In 1942 the Paras became part of the **Army Air Corps**, the other components being (briefly between 1944 and 1946) the Special Air Service and The Glider Pilot Regiment. The latter was formed in 1941 and played a distinguished role in wartime airborne operations, including the seizure of Pegasus Bridge over the Caen Canal in Normandy in June 1944, although Major John Howard's glider-borne infantry were from D Company, 2nd Battalion, The Oxfordshire and Buckinghamshire Light Infantry. Pegasus was the winged horse of the Greek hero Bellerophon, who slew the monster Chimaera, and the emblem of Bellerophon on Pegasus had been chosen for the Paras by Browning in 1941. The Paras and The Glider Pilot Regiment became part of The Glider Pilot and Parachute Corps in 1950, but this was discontinued in 1957 when the independent status of The Parachute Regiment was revived and a new **Army Air Corps** incorporating The Glider Pilot Regiment was formed. There are currently three battalions of Paras and six regiments within the Army Air Corps.

A pontoon section of 2/1st Company, Royal Engineers at Tonbridge in 1915 'resting after lifting and packing the pontoon on trolley'.

11. Corps and supporting services

The fighting or 'teeth' arms of an army have always depended upon a wide variety of supporting services and, increasingly through the twentieth century, the proportion of soldiers in teeth arms declined as more and more sophisticated support services were required in order to enable a modern highly mechanised army to fight efficiently.

Ranking immediately behind the **Royal Regiment of Artillery** in precedence, the oldest corps in the British Army is the **Corps of Royal Engineers**. A corps was first formed by the Master General of the Ordnance in August 1717, exclusively of officers, although they were not granted regular commissions until 1757. It was then only in March 1772 that a company of military artificers was raised at Gibraltar, the siege of the Rock by the Spanish between 1779 and 1783 proving their worth in co-operation with the artillery. Artificer companies were added to the home establishment in 1786, and in 1787 royal charters were granted for a Corps of Royal Engineers and a Corps of Royal Military Artificers. The artificers were renamed the Royal Sappers and Miners in 1813, and it was only in 1856 that the two separate corps for officers and men were combined as the Corps of Royal Engineers.

Like the artillery, the engineers were more professional than the other arms through their need to master their duties. Siege warfare, surveying, bridging and civil and military construction were engineering duties from the start, but those duties became ever wider through new developments such as the railway, electric telegraph, steam tractors, submarine diving and mining, balloons, searchlights and aircraft. A permanent Balloon Section, for example, was formed in 1890 and an air battalion in 1911, the latter becoming the nucleus of the Royal Flying Corps in April 1912. The balloon factory established at Chatham in 1887 was moved to Aldershot in 1892 and to Farnborough in 1906, later the home of the Royal Aircraft Establishment. There were few campaigns in which engineers did not make their mark and since, like the artillery, they carried no Colours it was appropriate that their battle honour should be *Ubique* ('Everywhere'). It was from the signal companies of the engineers that a separate **Royal Corps of Signals** was created in 1920, the new corps adopting the symbol of Mercury, winged messenger of the Greek gods, as its badge.

A driver of the Army Service Corps with his pair of draught horses in 'review order' prior to the First World War.

Rather as early artillerymen were civilians, so the army's transport was long the responsibility of the civilian Commissariat, various Commissaries General being appointed on an ad hoc basis for campaigns until the department was regularised in 1806. However, the Commissariat was under direct Treasury control from 1816 until 1854, a factor contributing to the woeful state of the department during the Crimean War. There had been a Corps of Waggoners, later the Royal Waggon Train, from 1794 to 1833 and, under the strains of the breakdown of supply services in the Crimea, a new Land Transport Corps was hastily created in 1855. This was converted into the Military Train in 1857, the Control Department and Army Service Corps in 1870 and the Commissariat and Transport Corps in 1881. However, its officers held military rank only within the corps itself. As a result of the initiative of Sir Redvers Buller when Adjutant-General, an Army Service Corps was created in 1888 to bring the corps fully into the army's establishment, the title of Royal Army Service Corps being granted in 1918. The RASC then became The Royal Corps of Transport in 1965. The Royal Army Ordnance Corps also received its royal title in 1918, this being a union of the officers of the Army Ordnance Office, dating from 1881 but with origins in the Military Store Staff Corps of 1875, and the other ranks of the Ordnance Store Branch, formed in 1877. The Royal Pioneer Corps was so named in 1946, having originated as the Auxiliary Military Pioneer Corps in 1939 although there had been a Labour Corps during the First World War. Together with the Army Catering Corps, formed in 1941, and the Royal Engineers (Postal

Appropriately, the badge of the Royal Pioneer Corps included a spade, pick-axe and rifle with the motto 'Labor omnia vincit' ('Work conquers all').

55

and Courier Service), the RCT, RAOC and RPC were brought together in April 1993 as the **Royal Logistic Corps**.

The other new corps, formed a year earlier in April 1992, was the **Adjutant General's Corps**, comprising the Royal Army Pay Corps (1870), the Military Provost Staff Corps (1901), the Royal Army Educational Corps (1920), the Royal Military Police (1946), the Women's Royal Army Corps (1949) and the Army Legal Corps (1978). Of these, the Royal Military Police have their origins in the Military Mounted Police of 1877 and the Military Foot Police of 1885 while the RAPC can trace its origins to the Pay Sub-department of the Control Department in 1870. Still remaining as separate corps are the **Royal Army Medical Corps** (1898), the **Royal Army Veterinary Corps** (1918), the **Royal Army Chaplains' Department** (1919), the **Royal Army Dental Corps** (1921), the **Small Arms School Corps** (1929), the **Intelligence Corps** (1940), the **Army Physical Training Corps** (1940) and the **Royal Electrical and Mechanical Engineers** (1942).

Some of these corps, too, have earlier antecedents. The **Small Arms School Corps**, for example, began as the School of Musketry at Hythe in 1853, taking in the Machine Gun School at Netheravon in 1923. There have been chaplains with the army since 1796 while the **Royal Army Medical Corps** can trace its origins to the Army Hospital Corps of 1857. Both doctors and chaplains have performed extraordinary feats of heroism, two of the three men to be awarded a bar to the Victoria Cross being doctors: Arthur Martin-Leake, whose first award came in the South African War and his second in the First World War, and Noel Chavasse, who won both his awards in the First World War; the third man is the New Zealander Charles Upham, who won his VC and bar in the Second World War. One of the most remarkable accounts of the experience of soldiers in the First World War, *The War the Infantry Knew*, published in 1938, was also the work of a regimental medical officer, Captain James Churchill Dunn, RAMC, attached to 2nd Battalion, The Royal Welch Fusiliers (or Royal Welsh Fusiliers as the regiment was then designated) from November 1915 to May 1918.

Surgeon Major Martin-Leake of the Royal Army Medical Corps, who won the Victoria Cross in the South African War and again in the First World War. (Illustration from 'The Victoria Cross' by Peter Duckers, Shire, 2005.)

12. Establishments

The origin of most modern military academies lay in the need for professional training for officers of artillery and engineers. Thus, the United States Military Academy, West Point, began as an artillery and engineering school in 1802, as did the École Polytechnique in France in 1795. The latter was first founded at Mézières in 1749 and was directly modelled on the Royal Military Academy, Woolwich, established in April 1741, although the French had had an artillery school since 1679 and Prussia an engineering school since 1706. Known as 'The Shop', Woolwich was intended to instruct 'raw and inexperienced people.... in the several parts of Mathematiks necessary to qualify them for the Service of the Artillery, and the business of Engineers'. Originally in the Warren (now the Royal Arsenal), the academy moved to Woolwich Common in 1806. Until 1761 cadets were commissioned in the artillery and then transferred if they wished to the engineers but thereafter were commissioned direct into both corps. Woolwich remained the main route to a commission in the **Royal Artillery** and **Royal Engineers** until the outbreak of the Second World War.

As Commander-in-Chief, the Duke of York was determined to raise professional standards, and in 1799 a Royal Military College was founded, comprising initially a senior or staff department at the Antelope Inn in High Wycombe, Buckinghamshire, under the command of a French émigré, Francis Jarry, and, from 1802, a junior department at Remnantz in nearby Marlow under Lieutenant Colonel (later Major-General) John Le Marchant, who was killed at the head of Wellington's Heavy Cavalry Brigade at the Battle of Salamanca in July 1812. The senior department moved out to Farnham in 1813 while the junior department was moved to a new site at Sandhurst on the Berkshire/Surrey border in 1812, where the senior department also moved eight years later. In 1809 the Military Seminary at Addiscombe was also opened for cadets wishing to enter the service of the East India Company; Addiscombe closed in 1861, and thereafter cadets for the British Indian Army went to Sandhurst or

Woolwich depending upon arm of service. In January 1947 Woolwich was closed and officer training was consolidated at what was now to be the **Royal Military Academy, Sandhurst**. A relatively recent custom observed in the Passing Out Parades at Sandhurst is for the Academy Adjutant, who commands the parade, to ride his horse up the steps of the Academy's Grand Entrance at the conclusion, following the graduating cadets who march up in slow time to the tune *Auld Lang Syne*. It was begun by 'Boy' Browning, whose contribution to

The Royal Military Academy building in the grounds of the former Royal Arsenal at Woolwich, London.

the development of airborne forces is described in Chapter 10, when he was Adjutant in 1924.

Standards at Woolwich and Sandhurst were not initially high despite the employment of civilian staff such as the artist Paul Sandby and the scientist Michael Faraday at Woolwich and the eminent mathematician John Narrien at Sandhurst. Indeed, a Select Committee on Sandhurst was especially critical in 1855, leading to new competitive examinations for both Woolwich and Sandhurst and the revitalisation of the senior department as the Staff College, Camberley, in 1858. However, it was many years before the Staff College established itself as the prerequisite for advancement to the army's highest ranks. In 1996 the Staff College moved out of Camberley to be combined with the former Royal Air Force Staff College and the former Royal Naval College, Greenwich, at Bracknell as the **Joint Services Command and Staff College**.

Many famous soldiers of the nineteenth and twentieth centuries passed through Woolwich or Sandhurst, but one who is especially commemorated at Sandhurst (as successor to Woolwich) is Louis Napoleon, the Prince Imperial of France and son of the Emperor Napoleon III. After the fall of the Second Empire in 1870 the imperial family moved to England. Louis graduated from Woolwich in 1875, but it was politically impossible for him to be offered a commission. Allowed to join the British forces in Zululand in an unofficial capacity, the Prince was killed in controversial

The death of Louis Napoleon, Prince Imperial of France, at the hands of the Zulus on 31st May 1879 while serving with the British forces. He had graduated from the Royal Military Academy, Woolwich.

circumstances on a reconnaissance on 31st May 1879. The Prince is buried in St Michael's Abbey, Farnborough, alongside his father, but artefacts connected with him are on display at Sandhurst and there is a fine statue that was moved to the Academy from Woolwich in 1947.

The establishment of the School of Musketry at Hythe in 1853 has been mentioned in Chapter 11. In 1852 an engineering school of instruction was established at Chatham in succession to the earlier Royal Engineer Establishment and an artillery school at Shoeburyness. All three establishments were the product of reforms introduced by Lord Hardinge as Commander-in-Chief. Hardinge also oversaw the holding of a 'camp of exercise' at Chobham in 1853, and land was purchased at Aldershot to provide a more permanent site for manoeuvres, this being the origin of Aldershot as the 'home of the British Army'. The **Royal Military School of Music** was opened at Kneller Hall in 1857, the Army Medical College at Chatham in 1859 and the Military Veterinary School at Aldershot in 1880. Later establishments include the School of Infantry, opened at Warminster in 1945, the Army Signal School, originally opened at Aldershot in 1905 and moved to Catterick in 1924, and the Armoured Fighting Vehicle School at Bovington.

The statue of Louis Napoleon erected at Woolwich, paid for by a subscription fund to which officers and other ranks alike contributed. It was moved to Sandhurst in 1947.

This window at Chearsley church in Buckinghamshire commemorates a former Lord Lieutenant, Sir Henry Floyd. It includes the badges of the 15th/19th Hussars (left) and the Honourable Corps of Gentlemen at Arms (right).

13. Veterans

Mention has already been made of a number of corps reserved for ex-servicemen, former officers serving in the **Honourable Corps of Gentlemen at Arms** and the **Royal Company of Archers of Scotland** and former soldiers in the **Yeomen of the Guard** and the **Yeomen Warders of the Tower of London**. Mention should also be made of the **Military Knights of Windsor**, comprising a Governor and seventeen Knights, all of whom are retired officers, the corps being originally established by Edward III (1327-77) and then revived by Elizabeth I in 1559. Former soldiers also serve in the **Corps of Commissionaires**, a private organisation founded in 1859 as a means of employment for former soldiers.

The need for a private organisation to provide employment for ex-servicemen was testimony to the remarkably poor provision afforded veterans in former times. Some provision was made for the relief of disabled soldiers under Elizabeth I, but the best-known foundation for veterans is the **Royal Hospital, Chelsea**, established by Charles II in February 1682 for those soldiers who had become unfit for duty after twenty years' service or as a result of wounds. A similar establishment had been authorised for the Irish Army at Kilmainham near Dublin in October 1679, Charles consciously imitating the Hôtel des Invalides, which Louis XIV of France had founded in Paris in 1670. According to legend, it was Nell Gwynne who inspired the creation of Chelsea, but the Duke of Monmouth, Charles's illegitimate son, had

Kilmainham Hospital, Dublin.

Chelsea Pensioners at a parade service at the Royal Hospital in 1996.

twice visited the Invalides and reported on it. The Pensioners still celebrate Oak Apple Day (29th May), Charles II's birthday, in their Founder's Day Parade with each pensioner wearing oak leaves on his tunic. Full dress is a scarlet coat with blue facings and tricorn hat reminiscent of the infantry uniform of the early eighteenth century, and the Hospital's calls are still by beat of drum rather than bugle.

The Royal Hospital, which was designed by Sir Christopher Wren, was not completed until 1690, and the first In-Pensioners were admitted in 1692. Initially the establishment was fixed at eight officers and 412 other ranks, but for much of the eighteenth century it was twenty-six officers and 450 other ranks, with a further three officers and sixty men added in 1816 and another thirty men in 1850. Currently there are about 450 Chelsea Pensioners – single men or widowers of good character and normally not less than sixty-five years of age. The term In-Pensioner differentiated those resident at Chelsea from those otherwise eligible but for whom no place could be found. The latter were therefore Out-Pensioners and in the seventeenth century were organised into Invalid Companies for garrison duties at Chester, Teignmouth, Hampton Court and Windsor, with further Out-Pensioners receiving a cash allowance in their own homes. In-Pensioners were also expected to undertake guard duties, maintaining an armed night patrol between 1715 and 1805 on the then rural road between the Hospital and St James's known as The King's Private Road, a haunt of highwaymen and footpads. In wartime Out-Pensioners were commonly formed into Invalid, Veteran and Garrison companies and, indeed, the 41st Foot, later 1st Battalion, The Welch Regiment, was formed in 1719 as an invalid battalion, only becoming a 'marching' line regiment in 1787. Other veterans' battalions were briefly organised between 1819 and 1821, and some ex-servicemen were encouraged to form military settlements in the colonies, although this idea was felt less promising after that drawn from veterans of the 91st Foot, later 1st Battalion, The Argyll and Sutherland Highlanders, who had taken their discharge in South Africa, was overwhelmed in the Eighth Cape Frontier (Kaffir) War in December 1850. In 1843 the various invalid companies were reorganised as Enrolled Pensioners, but they were absorbed into the army reserve in 1867.

Curiously, the Commissioners of Chelsea Hospital were responsible for the distribution of army prize money in the nineteenth century, the idea being that any remaining unclaimed after six years would be available for the use of the Hospital. Until 1847, when the Hospital was supported by Parliamentary votes, it had survived on various deductions from army pay and pensions.

14. Women in uniform

In earlier periods there were cases of women who disguised themselves as men – it was a favourite theme in folk song – and enlisted. Those who wrote memoirs in the eighteenth century included Hannah Snell, who served in the **Royal Marines** for five years, and Mary Anne Talbot, while in 1740 Daniel Defoe published an account of Christian Davies, better known as 'Mother Ross', who supposedly enlisted in the Royal Scots Greys to follow her husband and whose identity was discovered when she was wounded at Ramillies in May 1706. However, women associated with armies were usually encountered as 'camp followers', a general term which encompassed women acting as sutlers, wives, cooks, nurses, seamstresses, laundresses and prostitutes. Indeed, there were few armies without such followers, who shared the hardship of campaign such as the retreat to Corunna in the winter of 1808-9.

However, as armies became more professional so there was more regulation of the role of women, and, indeed, of children, as the morality of soldiers became a more significant consideration for society. Curiously, however, from 1837 until 1873 British soldiers remained exempt from the obligation placed on civilian males in 1834 to maintain their wives and children, and even then could not be punished for failing to do so for another ten years. In barracks, which only became permanent features of military life in Britain at the end of the eighteenth century, four married women per troop or company were allowed to live in the curtained corner of a barrack hut, with the others forced out into lodgings, and it was not until the mid nineteenth century that married quarters began to be provided, the first being for the Foot Guards in 1851. When the regiment proceeded on foreign service, the official number of wives permitted was six per company, with the exception of service in India and New South Wales when twelve per company were permitted. Those selected were chosen by lot, although it is clear the regulations were often flouted. However, while separation allowances were paid to militia wives, there was no systematic provision for the wives of regulars until the Crimean War and no allowances stipulated in army regulations until 1871.

Military nursing is inextricably linked with the Crimea and with the efforts of Florence Nightingale, superintendent of the Hospital for Invalid Gentlewomen in Harley Street, who offered her services to the government in October 1854 following the revelations of the poor medical conditions in the army by the war correspondent of *The Times*, W. H. Russell. The formidable Miss Nightingale was based at Scutari in Turkey and did not go to the Crimea

The 'Lady with the Lamp': the formidable Florence Nightingale as commemorated in London.

itself until May 1855, whereas others nursed in the Crimea. Miss Nightingale then became general superintendent of the 'female nursing establishment of the military hospitals of the army' in March 1856 although female nurses were not subsequently employed in military hospitals in large numbers until 1884 except at the Herbert Hospital, Woolwich, and the Royal Victoria Hospital, Netley. However, seven nurses were sent to South Africa in 1879, and another thirty-five served in Egypt and the Sudan between 1882 and 1885. The Army Nursing Service was eventually established in 1897, becoming Queen Alexandra's Imperial Nursing Service in 1902 and **Queen Alexandra's Royal Army Nursing Corps** in 1949. A Territorial Force Nursing Service was established in 1908, and this was augmented after 1909 by locally organised Voluntary Aid Detachments (VADs), which became part of the Territorial Technical Reserve and included large numbers of women. The quasi-aristocratic **First Aid Nursing Yeomanry** (FANY) was also formed in 1907 but had no connection to the actual yeomanry: it received official recognition in 1927.

There was a continuing reluctance to use women in any other capacity, but their work in the munitions industry during the First World War persuaded the War Office to reconsider, and in April 1915 the enrolment of cooks and waitresses was authorised, a Women's Legion receiving official recognition in February 1916. If women could replace men at home, then there was no logical reason why they could not do so abroad, and in March 1917 the first cooks from a new Women's Army Auxiliary Corps (WAAC) arrived in France although their status remained somewhat ambiguous: they had no military ranks and, instead of officers, had controllers and administrators. Eventually there were 41,000 women in the WAAC, renamed Queen Mary's Army Auxiliary Corps in September 1918. The latter was discontinued after the end of the war, but in September 1938 women were once more enrolled in what was now called the Auxiliary Territorial Service (ATS), which reached a strength of 212,500 in 1943. In February 1949 a new Women's Royal Army Corps (WRAC) was formed, this being absorbed into the **Adjutant General's Corps** in 1992, although a number of WRAC personnel were 're-badged' in other units such as the **Royal Corps of Signals** and the **Royal Logistic Corps**. In both the ATS and the WRAC, since Queen Elizabeth (now the Queen Mother) was Commandant-in-Chief, the Loyal Toast to George VI was followed by that of 'Our Commandant-in-Chief, The Queen'. Queen Elizabeth II, then HRH Princess Elizabeth, was commissioned in the ATS in March 1945.

The memorial in Whitehall, London, to 'The Women of World War II' was erected in 2006.

15. Ranks and appointments

There can sometimes be a distinction within military ranks between actual rank and appointment. Brigadier-general, for example, was an appointment and not a rank before the twentieth century so that normally the holder would be classed as colonel (temporary or local brigadier-general) and take precedence from the date of his promotion to colonel. Local or temporary rank in itself applied to a specific command or country in which it had effect. Rank could also be honorary – usually granted on retirement – or brevet. Brevet rank promotions were used to reward gallantry or special service and were permanent as regards precedence, but those with brevet rank remained at their original rank within their own regiment. Precedence itself was originally by seniority of regiment, but in 1690 William III directed that command should be taken according to seniority of commissions unless officers held commissions of the same rank and date, in which case seniority of regiment applied.

Until 1871 the majority of commissions in the infantry and cavalry were purchased, purchase being a system introduced during the reign of Charles II. However, it applied only up to the rank of colonel, after which merit and selection were applied. An official tariff and other regulatory measures were introduced in 1720 but, on occasions, could be flouted. There were abuses: James O'Hara, later second Lord Tyrawley, for example, was commissioned in the 7th Foot, later The Royal Fusiliers, at the age of thirteen in 1703 and succeeded his father as Colonel at the age of twenty-three while Lord George Lennox was also commissioned at the age of thirteen and was a lieutenant colonel in the 33rd Foot, now 3rd Battalion, **The Yorkshire Regiment (Duke of Wellington's)**, in 1758 at the age of only twenty. Lord Lucan's purchase of the command of the 17th Lancers in 1826 exceeded the official tariff by almost £19,000 and that of the 11th Hussars by his brother-in-law, Lord Cardigan, in 1836 by almost £34,000. Nonetheless, officers without means could find advancement although their promotion was likely to be slow, hence the apocryphal toast to a 'bloody war or a sickly season', since regiments serving overseas and on campaign had to fill vacancies rapidly from those available. Also, as officers purchased their commissions, they were thereby purchasing a stake in the political status quo and did not require pensions since they could sell their commissions on retirement. In 1793 it was laid down that no one under sixteen could purchase a first commission and no subaltern could advance to captain in less than two years and no officer to major or lieutenant colonel with less than six years' service. When purchase was eventually abolished by Edward Cardwell, it cost some £8 million in compensation to those who had lost their financial investment in their commissions. Purchase never applied to commissions in the artillery or engineers, promotion there being strictly by seniority. After 1871 the system was one of promotion by seniority 'tempered' by selection on the grounds of merit.

As indicated earlier, colonelcies of regiments were once proprietary appointments since, from 1692 to 1855, the Colonel was responsible for clothing the regiment and, until 1854, there were profits to be made from the deductions made from soldiers' pay for 'necessaries'; to a lesser extent, Captains of companies also benefitted from the system. Some of the abuses were removed in 1783, but after 1854 Colonels still received allowances in lieu of the lost proprietary rights until 1881, when all emoluments were removed and the appointment of Colonel of a regiment became purely honorary.

The assault on Boer positions at Laing's Nek on 26th January 1881 during the First Boer War was the last battle in which ensigns carried the colours into action.

Some ranks have disappeared over the centuries. The original first commission in the infantry until 1871 would be to the rank of Ensign and in the cavalry to Cornet. From 1871 to 1877 the first commission in both cavalry and infantry was Sub-Lieutenant and Second Lieutenant thereafter. Both Ensign and Cornet signified standard-bearer and derived from the French *enseigne* and *cornette*. The fusilier regiments, having no company colours, had no ensigns, so they had First and Second Lieutenants instead. Although the title Second Lieutenant was abolished in the fusiliers in 1834, it was then revived to replace that of Sub-Lieutenant generally in 1877. The last junior subalterns to perform the original role of ensign in carrying the Colours in battle were Lieutenants Baillie and Peel of the 58th Foot, later 2nd Battalion, The Northamptonshire Regiment, who did so at the battle of Laing's Nek on 26th January 1881 during the First Boer War (1880-1): Baillie was wounded, and Peel carried both Regimental and Queen's Colours until he was tripped by an ant-bear hole, after which a sergeant carried the colours to safety in the belief that Peel was dead. Baillie was then killed while being rescued by Lieutenant Hill, who received the Victoria Cross for this and for rescuing two other wounded men. The hoofs of Hill's horse were later mounted in silver as ashtrays for the officer's mess of the 58th while the Colours are in the National Army Museum. In the same battle, an old Etonian, Lieutenant Elwes of the **Grenadier Guards**, famously shouted to a fellow old Etonian, whose horse had been shot under him, Lieutenant Monck of the 58th, 'Come along Monck! *Floreat Etona*! We must be in the front rank.' Elwes was killed almost immediately, but Monck survived. The incident was celebrated in a famous painting by Lady Butler.

The rank of Captain-Lieutenant became that of Captain in 1772, with the earlier title abolished altogether in 1802. Similarly, the title of Major-General was originally that of Sergeant-Major-General and that of Major was originally Sergeant-Major, while Field Marshal emerged as a rank only in 1736 with the appointments of the first Earl of Orkney and the second Duke of Argyll. However, the rank was awarded only sparingly until the reign of Queen Victoria, when it became an almost routine recognition for old and distinguished soldiers. Officially, field marshals never retire, but there have been removals because the rank has been awarded to foreign sovereigns

Kaiser Wilhelm II of Germany with Winston Churchill at army manoeuvres in 1913. The Kaiser was a British field marshal and Colonel-in-Chief of the 1st Royal Dragoons.

whose states have subsequently gone to war with Britain. At the outbreak of the First World War, for example, both Kaiser Wilhelm II of Germany and Emperor Franz Joseph of Austria-Hungary were British field marshals, dating respectively from 1901 and 1903. The Kaiser and the Emperor were also Colonels-in-Chief of British regiments, respectively the 1st Royal Dragoons and 1st King's Dragoon Guards. Indeed, the KDG had adopted an Austrian doubled-headed eagle as its badge in honour of the Emperor, who had become Colonel-in-Chief in 1896: it was dropped in 1915 and only readopted in 1937. The 14th King's Hussars had a Prussian eagle as their badge, dating from 1798, when they had been the 14th (The Duchess of York's Own) Regiment of Light Dragoons, the Duchess being also the Princess Royal of Prussia: they also abandoned the badge in 1915 but resumed it in 1931. A similar situation with regard to a field marshal also arose in the Second World War, Emperor Hirohito of Japan having been made one in 1930. Other overseas sovereigns honoured have included King Leopold I of the Belgians (1816), King William II of the Netherlands (1845), the King of Nepal (1960) and Emperor Haile Selassie of Ethiopia (1965).

The army's commanders-in-chief initially went under the title of Captain-General, the first being George Monck, appointed by Charles II in 1660, although the titles of Captain-General and Commander-in-Chief were somewhat interchangeable through the eighteenth century: the Duke of York was the last titled as Captain-General in 1799, having earlier been named both Field Marshal on the Staff and Commander-in-Chief. Some variation in title continued into the nineteenth century:

Field Marshal Sir John French.

R 154.

Sir John French pictured in full field marshal's uniform just before the First World War. French was commander-in-chief of the British Expeditionary Force in France and Flanders from August 1914 to December 1915. Subsequently, he was Lord Lieutenant of Ireland from 1918 to 1921. He was created Earl of Ypres in the latter year.

66

Sir Garnet (later Field Marshal Lord) Wolseley, depicted as a major-general when chosen to command the Ashanti expedition in 1873. Wolseley's efficiency inspired the character of the 'very model of the modern major-general' in Gilbert and Sullivan's operetta 'The Pirates of Penzance'.

Wellington was Commander-in-Chief 1827-8 and 1842-52, but Sir Rowland Hill (1828-42) and Lord Hardinge (1852-6) were officially Generals (or Field Marshals) on the Staff and popularly General (or Field Marshal) Commanding-in-Chief. The Duke of Cambridge (1856-95) was similarly named until 1888, when he received an official patent as Commander-in-Chief, and this title was retained for Lords Wolseley (1895-1901) and Roberts (1901-4). In 1904, however, the post was abolished and a Chief of the General Staff substituted. From 1909 to 1964 the army's senior appointment was Chief of the Imperial General Staff but it then reverted to Chief of the General Staff while the powers of the Chief of the Defence Staff, originally created in 1958, have increased within a unified Ministry of Defence. The War Office also disappeared as a separate ministry in 1964.

One form of rank not generally understood is warrant officer rank, which exists between those of officers and non-commissioned officers. Warrant rank was of long standing in the Royal Navy but, initially, was only granted within the army under exceptional circumstances. Troop-Quartermasters, Trumpeters and Kettledrummers, for example, were warrant officers in **The Life Guards** until 1799, but there were no further warrant ranks until the appointment of Conductors in the Army Service Corps in 1879, these being able to take post as officers on parade but not to join in salutes. Similarly, warrant officers were addressed as if they were officers by non-commissioned officers and men but were not saluted. Warrant rank was then extended to the rest of the army, some being specialist appointments. Warrant Officers, Class I included Conductors, 1st Class Staff Sergeant-majors and Regimental Corporal-majors in the Household Cavalry, Bandmasters, and 1st and 2nd Class Master Gunners in the Royal Artillery. Warrant Officers, Class II included 3rd Class Master Gunners, Quartermaster-sergeants, Staff Sergeants and Colour Sergeants.

16. Colours

Colours (the identifying flags carried by a regiment) once had a highly practical function in being visible rallying points in the smoke and confusion of battle. At the same time, they had a highly symbolic role in marking the position of the commander whether of army, regiment or company and, in this sense, derived from the personal banners and armorial bearings of the medieval knight. In the New Model Army, as with most armies in the seventeenth century, each company or troop carried a separate Colour, differentiated from each other within the same regiment by the addition of various devices.

Regiments were restricted to a maximum of three Colours during Queen Anne's reign and, in 1743, to two Colours, these being the King's or Queen's Colour based on the Union Flag and the Regimental Colour, which, under a Royal Warrant of 1751, was based on the regiment's old uniform facing colour. However, there is an echo of the older system in the Foot Guards, where company devices are still borne in rotation on the Sovereign's Colour as new Colours are issued; the Foot Guards also differ from other regiments in that the Union Flag is the basis for their Regimental Colours. Two regiments were granted a third Colour as a result of their role at the Battle of Assaye in India in September 1803 during the Second Maratha War (1802-5): the 74th Foot, later 2nd Battalion, The Highland Light Infantry, and the 78th Foot, later 2nd Battalion, The Seaforth Highlanders. The tradition of the 74th's Assaye Colour is still kept up in **The Royal Highland Fusiliers, 2nd Battalion, the Royal Regiment of Scotland**. In the same campaign, the 76th Foot, later 2nd Battalion, The Duke of Wellington's Regiment, were awarded a second set of honorary Colours for their assault on the fortress of Ali Ghar and subsequent advance on Delhi. All three regiments also bore an elephant badge on their Colours, but these additional Colours, which had been awarded by the East India Company rather than the British military authorities, and third Colours possessed by a few other regiments such as the 5th Foot, later The Royal Northumberland Fusiliers, and the 2nd Foot, later The Queen's Royal Regiment (West Surrey), were not borne on parade. Moreover, in 1835 William IV directed that no third colours should be displayed on any occasion, this

The colours of The Royal West Kent Regiment rest in All Saints' Church, Maidstone, Kent.

The Colour Party of the 4th Battalion, Oxfordshire and Buckinghamshire Light Infantry at Windsor on 19th June 1909. The 4th Battalion was a Territorial battalion and before 1908 had been the 2nd Volunteer Battalion of the Oxfordshire Light Infantry.

ruling being upheld by George V in 1933. The exception was the 76th, who were permitted to carry their Honorary Colours on parade.

The Royal Military Academy, Sandhurst, has both Sovereign's and Regimental Colours and, in addition, at the passing-out parades, the cadet company regarded as having performed the best in training is designated the Sovereign's Company and carries the Sovereign's Banner. George V originally presented the banner for the then Champion Company in 1918, but it was renamed the Sovereign's Company at the request of George VI. The Sovereign's Banner is lowered to no one except the sovereign. There is also a Sovereign's Company in the **Grenadier Guards**.

In the case of cavalry, Dragoon Guards carried a single crimson square standard and Dragoons a single swallow-tailed guidon (from the French *guydhomme*) while Hussars and Lancers carried neither after 1834, thus depriving the 19th Royal Hussars of its second Assaye Colour won when it was the 1st Bengal European Light Cavalry. In the Household Cavalry, three Regimental Standards are borne in addition to the Sovereign's Standard and are effectively squadron standards.

Since they continued to be borne in action until 1881, the Colours were frequently reminders of those actions from the holes and cuts they bore. As such they took on even greater significance and bore the regiment's battle honours and other distinctions. Thus, the Colours came to be regarded very much as the soul of the regiment, being appropriately blessed when adopted and 'laid up', usually in churches or cathedrals, with all due ceremony, although it was only in 1898 that it became compulsory to lay them up in churches or suitable public buildings. Prior to this, Colonels could dispose of them as they wished; for example, the Colours of the 3rd Battalion, 14th Foot, which were carried at Waterloo, are kept in the former home of the then Colonel, Sir Harry Calvert, at Claydon House in Buckinghamshire. The presentation of new Colours is also a matter of some ceremony, usually in the form of a 'drum-head' service to consecrate them, a service which dates at least from the sixteenth century. ('Drum-head' means a ceremony taking place in front of a regiment, the 'head' being the skin stretched across the top of the drum.)

More will be said of battle honours later, but the other distinctions borne on

Queen Victoria presenting new colours to the 93rd (Sutherland) Highlanders at a drum-head service in Queen's Park, Edinburgh, on 19th August 1871. Ten years later, the 93rd became the 2nd Battalion, Argyll and Sutherland Highlanders.

Regimental Colours were also often just as significant in terms of the regiment's past. The 18th Foot, later The Royal Irish Regiment, was the first to be granted an honorary badge, this being the Lion of Nassau with the words *Virtutis Namurcensis Proemium* (The Reward of Valour at Namur), which was awarded by William III for the regiment's gallantry at the siege of Namur in 1695 during the Nine Years War (1689-97). Later, the Standard of the 6th Inniskilling Dragoon Guards received a badge of a castle flying St George's flag as a result of their earlier defence of Enniskillen in 1689. The sphinx was awarded to several regiments that took part in the British expedition to Egypt in 1801 while, as with the Assaye regiments, others bore elephant or tiger badges to commemorate service in India. An elephant with the addition of the words 'Carnatic' and 'Mysore', for example, was borne by The Royal Dublin Fusiliers, marking two engagements in the long campaign against Hyder Ali of Mysore and his son, Tippoo Sahib, between 1780 and 1799. Tigers were borne, among others, by the 14th Foot, later 1st Battalion, The West Yorkshire Regiment, the 17th Foot, later The Royal Leicestershire Regiment, and the 67th Foot, later 2nd Battalion, The Royal Hampshire Regiment. The dragon denoting service in China could be found on the Colours of regiments such as The Cameronians (Scottish Rifles), The North Staffordshire Regiment and The Royal Berkshire Regiment. Naval crowns were also borne on the Colours of regiments who had served as marines.

The story of Melvill and Coghill carrying away the Queen's Colour from Isandlwana has been told in chapter 9, and the Queen's Colour of **2nd Battalion, the Royal Welsh (The Royal Regiment of Wales)** still bears a wreath to commemorate their action, but this is by no means the only such example. At Albuhera in May 1811 Ensign Walsh of The Buffs (The Royal East Kent Regiment) was killed and the King's Colour was taken up by Lieutenant Latham. Latham was repeatedly struck by a French hussar, losing his left arm in the process. Latham tried to use the staff itself as a weapon with his right arm but was felled, only to tear the Colour from the staff to hide it under his tunic. Latham survived, being found still clutching the Colour after the battle: fellow officers presented him with a gold medal, he was promoted Captain and given a pension for life, and the Prince Regent paid for surgery on Latham's face. At Gandamak in January 1842, during a disastrous retreat from Kabul in the First Afghan War (1838-42), Lieutenant Souter of the 44th, later 1st Battalion, The Essex Regiment, wrapped the Queen's Colour around his body under his tunic to conceal it during the regiment's last stand. The seriously wounded Souter was taken prisoner but kept the Colour hidden until he was later rescued.

17. Badges

In his entertaining collection of autobiographical essays, *Unofficial History*, Field Marshal Viscount Slim recounted the story of one of his soldiers when he was serving in the 9th (Service) Battalion, The Royal Warwickshire Regiment, in Mesopotamia during the First World War rallying the remainder at a desperate moment by crying, 'Show the — yer cap badges'. As Slim wrote, 'They had no cap badges for we wore Wolseley helmets, but they heard the only appeal that could have reached them – to their Regiment, the last hold of the British soldier when all else had gone.' It is a reminder that, like the Colours, regimental badges have a special symbolism, the more so since Colours have ceased to be carried in action and since badges rather than lace and facing colours on uniforms have become the primary means of distinguishing one regiment from another.

Badges were originally devices on the Regimental Colours but came to be incorporated on grenadier and fusilier caps in the eighteenth century and ultimately on the front plates of the shakos adopted by the infantry as a whole in the French Revolutionary and Napoleonic Wars although, initially, shako plates mostly bore the regiment's number or, in the case of light infantry and rifles, a bugle badge. With the adoption of service dress and thus the field service cap for both foreign and home service after the South African War, cap badges became the norm although, as suggested by Slim, not on tropical pattern helmets, where cloth patches were worn.

In many cases the cap badge reflected those badges borne on the Colours, but they nearly all represented some aspect of the regiment's past associations and awards. Thus, the tiger denoting Indian service appeared on the badges of The Royal Leicestershire Regiment, The Royal Hampshire Regiment and The York and Lancaster Regiment; the dragon for service in China on that of The Royal Berkshire Regiment; and the sphinx for Egyptian service on those of The Royal Lincolnshire Regiment, The South Wales Borderers, The Lancashire Fusiliers, The Gloucestershire Regiment and The East Lancashire Regiment. Service during the siege of Gibraltar between 1779 and 1783 was recognised by the incorporation of castles, sometimes with the addition of a key and usually with the word 'Gibraltar'. Examples are the badges of The Suffolk Regiment, The Dorset Regiment, The Essex Regiment and The Northamptonshire Regiment. The castle and key were the arms of Gibraltar, granted by King Ferdinand II of Spain in 1502. However, the castle on the badge of The Royal Inniskilling Fusiliers was that of Enniskillen, and it was Exeter Castle that was represented on the badge of The Devonshire Regiment. The dragon on the badge of The Buffs (Royal East Kent Regiment) was not for China but represented

Past royal connections are evident in the badge of the 3rd King's Own Hussars, incorporating the White Horse of Hanover, and that of the 3rd Carabiniers, incorporating the three plumes associated with the Prince of Wales.

71

While Sergeant Charles Ewart of the 2nd Dragoons (Royal Scots Greys) captured the eagle of the French 45th Infantry at Waterloo on 18th June 1815, Captain A. K. Clark of the 1st Royal Dragoons took that of the 105th Infantry. Subsequently, eagles featured on both regiments' badges.

the dragon supporter of the arms of Elizabeth I, who reviewed Thomas Morgan's Company raised in 1572 for service in the Netherlands and from which the Holland Regiment of 1665 traced its descent. However, the Buffs did serve in China, Private John Moyse of the regiment being immortalised in a poem by Francis Hastings Doyle, *The Private of the Buffs*, for his execution following his refusal to kowtow to a Chinese mandarin after capture in August 1860. The **Royal Marines** were awarded the globe badge by George IV in 1827 since, like the **Royal Artillery** and **Royal Engineers**, their service was global.

Royal associations are frequently linked to badges. The Lion of England was the badge of The King's Own Royal Regiment (Lancaster) while the White Horse of Hanover featured in the badges of The King's Regiment (Liverpool), The West Yorkshire Regiment and the 3rd King's Own Hussars. Prince of Wales's plumes were adopted by The Welch Regiment, The North Staffordshire Regiment, the 3rd Carabiniers (Prince of Wales's Dragoon Guards), the 10th Royal Hussars (Prince of Wales's Own) and the 12th Royal Lancers (Prince of Wales's). However, the single plume included in the badge of The Royal Sussex Regiment in 1901 was that of the French Royal Roussillon Regiment, which was defeated by the 35th Foot at the Battle of the Heights of Abraham before the city of Quebec in September 1759, the men pulling the white plumes from the hats of the French and sticking them in their own. Similarly, representations of captured French eagles featured in the badges of The Royal

Above left: *Supposedly the cry of King Alexander of Scotland when wounded by a stag in the thirteenth century, 'Cuidich'n Righ' ('Help to the King') became the motto of the Seaforth Highlanders, the King having been rescued by a forebear of the Earl of Seaforth.*

Above right: *The motto 'Or Glory', borne on the badge of the 17th/21st Lancers, was taken from Grey's Elegy and commemorates the death of Wolfe at Quebec in 1759. The dispatches bearing news of Wolfe's death to England were carried by the first commanding officer of the original forerunner of the 17th Lancers.*

The 28th Foot, later the Gloucester-shire Regiment, earning its unique 'back badge' at Alexandria on 21st March 1801. Suddenly attacked from the rear as well as the front, the regiment's rear rank about-faced and both attacks were beaten off.

Dragoons (1st Dragoons), The Royal Scots Greys (2nd Dragoons) and The Royal Irish Fusiliers, who captured one at Barossa in the Peninsula in March 1811. The Duke of Wellington's Regiment, which was the only regiment other than The Green Howards to bear the title of an individual who was not of royal blood, has Wellington's family crest, a lion bearing a banner, which symbolised the flag that the Duke's descendants have to present to the Sovereign annually as quit-rent (a rent paid by a freeholder as a token of service) for the nation's gift of Stratfield Saye House in Hampshire as a family estate.

Some regiments also carried battle honours other than Gibraltar or Egypt on the cap badges. The Middlesex Regiment (Duke of Cambridge's Own), for example, bore 'Albuhera', this battle also providing the regiment with its nickname of 'The Die Hards', the wounded Colonel Inglis having cried out to his men, 'Die hard, 57th, die hard'. The Somerset Light Infantry (Prince Albert's) bore that of 'Jellalabad', the Afghan fortress defended by the 13th Foot for five months in 1842 during the First Afghan War, the mural crown superscribed 'Jellalabad' being the gift of Queen Victoria.

Mottoes on badges included one on that of The Seaforth Highlanders, *Cuidich 'n Righ* ('Help to the King'), supposedly the cry of King Alexander of Scotland when wounded by a stag in the Forest of Mar in the thirteenth century. The king was rescued by Colin Fitzgerald, whose descendants became Earls of Seaforth. The motto *Or Glory* on the badge of the 17th/21st Lancers has its origins – as well as the death's head and crossbones – with the 17th Lancers. Its first commanding officer when it was Hale's Light Horse, Lieutenant Colonel Hale, had brought back the dispatches from Quebec announcing the death of Major-General James Wolfe at the moment of victory and wished to commemorate Wolfe. The association is with the words from Gray's *Elegy Written in a Country Churchyard* quoted by Wolfe on the night before the battle: 'The paths of glory lead but to the grave.' Wolfe was also commemorated by The Loyal North Lancashire Regiment with a black line in its lace and epaulettes. The Dorset Regiment's *Primus in Indis* commemorates its role in Robert Clive's victory at Plassey in June 1757, it having been the first King's regiment

The badge of the Devonshire and Dorset Regiment incorporates Exeter Castle, formerly used on the badge of the Devons, with the sphinx earned by the Dorsets in Egypt and their motto, 'Primus in Indis', reflecting the service of the 39th Foot in India from 1754 to 1758 and its presence at the Battle of Plassey on 22nd June 1757.

Wearing pre-First World War full dress uniform, this sergeant of the Sherwood Foresters has additional arm badges showing that he was the sergeant of the best shooting company in the regiment (lower right arm) and had qualified as a marksman (lower left arm) and a gymnastics instructor (upper right arm).

THE SHERWOOD
FORESTERS.
(Notts & Derby Regt)

Sergeant.

to serve in India. The unique 'back badge' was worn by The Gloucestershire Regiment on the back of the cap to recall the Battle of Alexandria in March 1801 when the 28th Foot were attacked from the rear and the rear rank faced about to beat off the French. The 61st, who were linked with the 28th in 1881, had fought in the same campaign and wore the sphinx, with the result that the back badge became a sphinx in the new regiment.

The grouping of infantry regiments in 'brigades' in 1958 led to some attempt to impose common brigade badges, but this was discontinued when the brigade structure was abandoned ten years later. Inevitably, however, further reductions have resulted in the appearance of new badges that have attempted to combine elements of the former regiments. The Devonshire and Dorset Regiment, for example, combined the castle of Exeter from The Devonshire Regiment with the sphinx and *Primus in Indis* motto of The Dorset Regiment. **The Royal Anglian Regiment** preserves the castle commemorating Gibraltar, which was previously borne by three of its component regiments, The Suffolk Regiment, The Essex Regiment and The Northamptonshire Regiment, but, while its star background is loosely reminiscent of another component, The Bedfordshire and Hertfordshire Regiment, there is no resemblance to the old badges of the remaining components, The Royal Norfolk Regiment, The Royal Lincolnshire Regiment and The Royal Leicestershire Regiment.

Arm badges are also worn primarily in cavalry regiments. Initially, these were rank badges for non-commissioned and warrant officers, but the 15th King's Light Dragoons, later 15th The King's Hussars, adopted a gold embroidered crown above the rank chevrons in 1801, and the practice became widespread and embraced other regimental symbols, both embroidered and in metal. NCOs of the 1st King's Dragoon Guards, for example, wore an embroidered Austrian eagle, the 3rd Dragoon Guards wore the Prince of Wales's plumes, the 8th King's Royal Irish Hussars a winged harp and so on. The 14th/20th King's Hussars originally had a Prussian eagle but also adopted crossed *kukris* in 1947 to commemorate its association during the Italian campaign in the Second World War with the 43rd Gurkha Lorried Infantry Brigade; the 6th Queen Elizabeth's Own Gurkha Rifles similarly adopted an eagle badge. Various specialised functions have also been reflected in arm badges for such men as farriers (a horseshoe), armourers (hammer and pincers), pipers (pipes), pilots (wings) and so on. In both world wars, cloth divisional formation signs were also worn on khaki battledress such as the crossed keys of the 2nd Division, the wyvern of the 43rd (Wessex) Division and the red jerboa (or desert rat) of the 7th Armoured Division.

Some mottoes borne on Colours and badges were relatively conventional, *Honi soit qui mal y pense* ('Let him who thinks evil of it be ashamed') being that of several regiments including the **Coldstream Guards**, The Royal Warwickshire Regiment, The King's Liverpool Regiment, The Lancashire Fusiliers, The Somerset Light Infantry and The Royal Berkshire Regiment. *Ich Dien* ('I serve') was common to several including The Royal Irish Fusiliers, The Prince of Wales's Leinster Regiment (Royal Canadian), The Middlesex Regiment and The North Staffordshire Regiment. However, The Suffolk Regiment, The Northamptonshire Regiment and The Essex Regiment all had *Montis insignia Calpe* ('The badges of Gibraltar' – since Gibraltar is Mount Calpe), and The King's Royal Rifle Corps was granted *Celer et audax* ('Swift and bold') for distinguished service in North America in 1759 (though not until 1824).

The memorial to the 2nd Battalion, The Worcestershire Regiment, commemorating its charge at Gheluvelt in October 1914 that turned the tide at a crucial moment in the First Battle of Ypres.

18. Customs

Regimental customs arise for a variety of reasons. Some clearly reflect particular past episodes. In The Cameronians (The Scottish Rifles), for example, the Covenanter past of the 26th Foot was remembered by posting picquets on commanding heights whenever divine service was held in the open air because the followers of Richard Cameron, who was executed in 1680, were not safe from attack by James II's forces even at prayer. The regiment held an annual Conventicle on the nearest Sunday to 12th May, the anniversary of their acceptance into the army by William III, when the watch was kept in case the king proved treacherous. The Cameronians also carried their rifles into church and went to church parade unaccompanied by music, reflecting the secrecy with which religious gatherings originally had to be held. When the regiment chose disbandment in 1968 it did so with a Conventicle on 12th May. Similarly, officers of the 29th Foot, later 1st Battalion, The Worcestershire Regiment, always wore swords at mess following an attack by supposedly loyal North American Indians while officers were at dinner in September 1746. Subsequently, the tradition was maintained after 1842 by the orderly officer of the day and the captain of the week alone wearing their swords.

The Cameronians also proposed the Loyal Toast but did not drink it since Presbyterians were abstainers. Some other regiments also did not drink the Loyal Toast, usually claiming that they had been given special permission not to do so by a past sovereign. This was certainly the case for the 85th Foot, later 2nd Battalion, The King's Shropshire Light Infantry, since George IV rewarded the regiment for protecting him during a disturbance at Brighton by telling the officers they need not drink his health nor stand when the National Anthem was played. Others who did not drink the Loyal Toast on less sure grounds included the 3rd Carabiniers, the 3rd Hussars and The Royal Fusiliers while the 32nd Foot, later 1st Battalion, The Duke of Cornwall's Light Infantry, drank it only once a year on the Sovereign's birthday in commemoration of their defence of Lucknow during the Indian Mutiny, when wine was in short supply. Some regiments that had served as marines drank the Loyal Toast sitting down in reference to the practice in the Royal Navy, originally because of the low beams in naval vessels. There were also several variations in how the Loyal Toast was actually proposed while some regiments immediately followed it with regimental toasts, such as in the 51st Foot, later 1st Battalion, The King's Own Yorkshire Light Infantry, where the second toast was to 'Ensign Dyas and the Stormers', commemorating Dyas's gallantry leading storming parties at the siege of Badajoz. The 45th Foot, later 1st Battalion, The Sherwood Foresters (Nottinghamshire and Derbyshire Regiment), commemorated the actual fall of the fortress to Wellington's army on Badajoz Day (6th April). Despite being badly wounded, Lieutenant Macpherson seized the French flag flying above the castle and replaced it with his tunic: thereafter, the regiment flew a scarlet jacket from the flagstaff on Badajoz Day, and the tradition is kept up in **2nd Battalion, The Mercian Regiment (Worcesters and Foresters)**.

Other days specially kept by regiments included 'Oates Sunday' in the 5th Royal Inniskilling Dragoon Guards, the nearest Sunday to 17th March being observed in memory of the birthday of Captain L. E. G. Oates, who died on Captain Scott's Antarctic expedition in 1912; fearing he had become a burden, Oates left the shelter of the party's tent to certain death in the blizzard outside. Minden Day (1st August) was celebrated by five of the six regiments who, misinterpreting their orders, advanced on a mass of French cavalry at this Seven Years War battle on the banks of the Weser in Germany in 1759 and put them to flight. As they advanced through an area full of wild rose briars, the men put roses in their hats and uniforms. The 23rd, later The Royal Welch Fusiliers, did not mark the day, but the 12th (The Suffolk

The 51st Foot, later the 1st Battalion, The King's Own Yorkshire Infantry, was one of six British infantry battalions that broke a superior force of French cavalry while advancing through an area of wild rose briars at Minden on 1st August 1759.

Regiment), the 20th (The Lancashire Fusiliers), the 25th (The King's Own Scottish Borderers), the 37th (1st Battalion, The Royal Hampshire Regiment) and the 51st (1st Battalion, The King's Own Yorkshire Light Infantry) thereafter wore roses in their hats on Minden Day, while in The Lancashire Fusiliers red and yellow roses also decorated the drums and any officer who had not previously done so would eat a rose from a silver finger bowl filled with champagne. Red and white roses were also worn in The Royal Northumberland Fusiliers on St George's Day (23rd April) since St George slaying the dragon had been a regimental badge from an early period although the regiment actually began in 1674 as an Irish regiment in Dutch service, transferring to the English establishment in 1688.

It might be argued that particular sports are also in the nature of military customs. Snooker, for example, is usually attributed to Sir Neville Chamberlain, who supposedly invented the game at Ootacamund in India. Polo was developed by Lieutenant (later Major-General) John Sherer, Bengal Native Infantry, and Captain Robert Stewart, the Superintendent of Cachar, in the late 1850s after seeing tribesmen in Manipur play *chaugan*. They brought it to Calcutta in 1864, and the 10th Hussars then brought the game to England in 1869; inter-regimental tournaments were instituted in both India (1877) and at home (1878). While polo is sometimes regarded exclusively as a cavalry sport, the Indian tournament was actually won three times in the 1890s by 2nd Battalion, Durham Light Infantry. Winston Churchill played in the winning team from the 4th Queen's Own Hussars in 1899 while Douglas Haig played regularly in the successful 7th Queen's Own Hussars Indian teams of the 1880s and led that of the 17th Lancers to victory in the home tournament in 1903. Also, military teams were among the first to take up football. The **Royal Engineers** team was one of the founders of the Football Association in 1863; they won the FA Cup in 1875 and were runners up in the first ever Cup Final, in 1872, as well as again in 1874 and 1878. Captain (later Major) Sir Francis Marindin of the Engineers was also President of the FA from 1874 to 1890. Rugby's Calcutta Cup was brought to England and presented to the Rugby Union by The Buffs (Royal East Kent Regiment).

The army carried football and cricket throughout the empire, and sport, not least field sports, was regarded as having an essential part to play in cultivating military virtues. On 1st July 1916 Captain W. P. Neville of the 8th (Service) Battalion, The East Surrey Regiment kicked off his company's attack across No Man's Land on the Somme, having bought a football for each of his platoons. Neville was killed almost instantly but contemporaries did not see anything remarkable in the link between sport and war. Lieutenant Colonel John Campbell of the **Coldstream Guards** was awarded a VC for rallying his men to undertake a counter-attack in one of the Somme engagements; a pre-war master of the Tanet Side Harriers, Campbell did so by sounding his hunting horn. On 29th August 1914 2nd Battalion, The Royal Sussex Regiment briefly halted on the retreat from Mons while the Colonel handed out the medals, which had only just arrived, to the winning company team in the regimental cricket cup.

The Shetland pony mascot of the Argyll and Sutherland Highlanders.

19. Mascots

British soldiers often acquired an extraordinary menagerie of animals when on service, and some became official mascots. One famous dog is 'Bobby', who was taken on by the 66th Foot, later 2nd Battalion, The Royal Berkshire Regiment, in Malta and then accompanied the regiment to India. At Maiwand in Afghanistan in July 1880, the 66th was reduced to just eleven men, who made their last stand near Khig. As depicted in a celebrated painting by Frank Feller, 'Bobby' stayed with them until they were overwhelmed. Later, blood-covered and with a slight bullet wound, she turned up at Kandahar. Taken home with the remnants of the regiment, she was presented to Queen Victoria, who awarded her the campaign medal. Sadly, 'Bobby' was run down by a hansom cab in Gosport but was stuffed and is still on show at the museum of The Royal Gloucestershire, Berkshire and Wiltshire Regiment. 'Bob', the terrier that accompanied the **Scots Guards** through the hardships of the Crimea, was also to be run down – by a butcher's cart – in London in 1860 and, similarly, stuffed, was once displayed in the Scottish United Services Museum in Edinburgh wearing the Crimean medal.

Among more unusual mascots were the bears favoured by the 17th Lancers, who had at least three in the Victorian period, and the blackbucks favoured by The Royal Warwickshire Regiment, who acquired its first in India in 1871 because its badge was an antelope. The Royal Dragoons had a goose called 'Jock' from 1921 to 1929. Rams and goats are more usual. In 1857 the 95th Foot, later 2nd Battalion, The Sherwood Foresters, acquired a ram at the fall of Kotah during the Indian Mutiny. The ram marched over 3000 miles with the regiment, being awarded the Mutiny medal. As they had been The Derbyshire Regiment since being raised in 1823, the ram was named 'Derby I' and each successor was numbered in turn: by 1970 the

*One of the long
succession of
regimental goats, all
named 'Billy', of the
Royal Welch Fusiliers,
pictured during the
First World War.*

regiment was being served by Derby XXI. Similarly, The Royal Welch Fusiliers had a succession of goats – always referred to as The Regimental Goat and never as a mascot – from at least the American War of Independence onwards, and The Welch Regiment from the 1850s. In the former the goat was always 'Billy' and in the latter always 'Taffy'. Upon amalgamation with The South Wales Borderers in 1969, the last goat of The Welch Regiment therefore became 'Taffy I' of The Royal Regiment of Wales (24th/41st Foot).

*The regimental
mascots of the
Staffordshire
Regiment
(Prince of
Wales's) are
Staffordshire
bull terriers,
named
'Watchman'.
They are
buried on the
green opposite
the town hall
at Burton upon
Trent.*

79

20. Nicknames

Several regiments have been given nicknames. Some are quite simply a play on the initials used as abbreviations for regiments or corps. Thus the **Royal Army Medical Corps** was 'Rob All My Comrades', the old Military Store Staff Corps, which had been a forerunner of the Royal Army Ordnance Corps, was 'My Sister Sells Cabbages', and the Army Service Corps was 'Ally Sloper's Cavalry'. The **Adjutant General's Corps**, incorporating the Women's Royal Army Corps, has quickly become 'The All Girls Corps'.

Other nicknames, however, are of older antecedence. Thus the 2nd Foot, later The Queen's Royal Regiment (West Surrey), were 'Kirke's Lambs', an ironic title both reflecting their brutality in suppressing the Monmouth rebellion in the West Country in 1685 while under the command of Percy Kirke and also referring to the Paschal Lamb badge. However, they were also known as 'The Tangerines' from their origin as a regiment raised for the garrison at Tangier. The 6th Foot, later The Royal Warwickshire Fusiliers, were once 'Guise's Geese' after their Colonel between 1738 and 1765, John Guise. The Queen's Bays (2nd Dragoon Guards) were 'The Rusty Buckles', supposedly from returning from service in Ireland in the eighteenth century to find that all other cavalry regiments had converted from steel accoutrements to brass.

Some nicknames were fairly obvious derivatives from the original numbered foot regiments such as 'The Fighting Ninth' (The Royal Norfolk Regiment), 'The Two Twos' (The Cheshire Regiment), 'The Two Fives' (The Border Regiment), 'The Excellers' (The South Lancashire Regiment) from the Roman numerals XL, and 'The Old Five and Three Pennies' (The King's Shropshire Light Infantry). The tiger badge from Indian service gave The Royal Leicestershire Regiment their alternative nicknames of 'Bengal Tigers' and 'The Tigers' while The Royal Lincolnshire Regiment was inevitably 'The Poachers' from the song, 'The Lincolnshire Poacher', which was also the regimental march.

The Sherwood Foresters earned their nickname of 'The Old Stubborns' at Talavera on 27th and 28th July 1809 when defending an outpost against a French mass attack. Still serving in the Peninsula, they again distinguished themselves at Salamanca on 22nd July 1812.

1st Battalion, The Duke of Wellington's Regiment colour party at the Changing of the Guard, Buckingham Palace, in 1999. The battalion is now part of The Yorkshire Regiment.

Less obvious nicknames included 'The Havecake Lads' for The Duke of Wellington's Regiment, supposedly because recruiting sergeants carried oatcakes on their swords as a means of attracting recruits, and 'The Bloodsuckers' (The Manchester Regiment), from the *fleur de lys* badge of the 63rd Foot, said to resemble the mosquitoes of the West Indies. Specific military exploits were recalled in 'The Emperor's Chambermaids' (14th King's Hussars), who had captured the coach of Napoleon's brother, Joseph Bonaparte, including its ornate chamberpot, after the Battle of Vittoria in June 1813; and 'The Delhi Spearmen' (9th Queen's Royal Lancers), gained from their exploits at the siege of Delhi in 1857. The nickname of 'The Bloody Eleventh' (The Devonshire Regiment) was a result of large casualties at Salamanca in July 1812, and 'The Old Stubborns' (The Sherwood Foresters) a result of gallantry at Talavera in July 1809.

21. Bands and marches

The first musicians – fifers and drummers in the infantry and trumpeters in the cavalry– attached to regiments were intended to convey commands in camp, on the march and in battle, even beating the time on the hour. Often negro bandsmen were added in the eighteenth century as a range of new percussion instruments were introduced, while bugles were first adopted by the light infantry regiments initially in the form of a horn. Later, bands of brass or woodwind instruments such as hautboys, horns and bassoons were added for both ceremony and entertainment, the ceremonies of Retreat and Tattoo (see next chapter) becoming general in the eighteenth century. Often, however, bandsmen were civilians hired by the regiment's officers, and the same was true of the bandmaster, Germans becoming particular favourites in the nineteenth century.

The bagpipes were not much favoured officially in Scottish regiments in the eighteenth century because of their associations with rebellious Highlanders. However, they soon became firmly established although they were only officially sanctioned for two regiments in 1854 and for all Highland regiments in 1881, when an establishment of five pipers was fixed. Lowland regiments were then authorised to have up to five pipers at regimental expense in 1884. It was not until 1918 that all Scottish regiments were permitted a Pipe-Major and six pipers, any additional pipers to be at regimental expense. The Army School of Piping was only established in 1910. However, Highland regiments also had military bands; one of the most famous British composers of military marches, Kenneth Alford, whose works include 'The Great Little Army' and 'Colonel Bogey', was bandmaster of The Argyll and Sutherland Highlanders. Irish regiments generally did not have pipes until the twentieth century .

Initially, bandsmen wore coats of the regimental facing colour, but during the French Revolutionary and Napoleonic Wars this practice ceased although drummers

A piper of the Black Watch just before the First World War.

From the war memorial of the King's Liverpool Regiment in Liverpool, this representation of a drummer in eighteenth-century uniform clearly illustrates the shoulder 'wings' still worn by drummers of the Foot Guards.

kept additional lace on their uniforms and 'wings' or flaps on the shoulders, still seen on the uniforms of drummers in the Foot Guards. Drum-Majors of the Foot Guards also still wear seventeenth-century-style ceremonial state dress, as do musicians of the Household Cavalry on state occasions. Rifles and light infantry naturally had Bugle-Majors rather than Drum-Majors, cavalry had Trumpet-Majors and Highland regiments had Pipe-Majors. Drums themselves are of the old facing colours of regiments and embellished with the regimental badge and battle honours while the Drum-Major's drum belt also bears badge and battle honours. In the cavalry, the drum banners of the kettle-drummer were similarly embellished although only the Household Cavalry now preserves the kettle-drummer. The 3rd The King's Own Hussars, however, did not have battle honours on their kettle-drum banners because, having captured the silver kettle-drums of a French regiment at Dettingen in June 1743, they engraved their honours on the drums themselves. The Trumpet-Major of the 5th Dragoon Guards (Princess Charlotte of Wales's) carried an infantry drum-major's staff captured from the French 66th Regiment at Salamanca in July 1812.

One of the earliest recorded regimental marches was 'Dumbarton's Drums', that of The Royal Scots, their third Colonel being Lord James Douglas, Earl of Dumbarton. It is thought that the march may have been the 'Scotch March' mentioned

Drummers of the Guards return down The Mall after Trooping the Colour.

Piper Findlater of the Gordon Highlanders winning the Victoria Cross at Dargai on the North-west Frontier on 20th October 1897. Findlater became a minor celebrity in Britain, but his subsequent financial difficulties, after being discharged as a result of his wounds, led to the annual annuity for VC winners being raised from £10 to £50 in 1898.

by Samuel Pepys in his diary after hearing it played by the regiment in Rochester in June 1667. Other marches using old traditional tunes included 'Come Lasses and Lads', a seventeenth-century tune adopted by The South Staffordshire Regiment, and 'D'Ye Ken John Peel', taken up by The Border Regiment. The Royal Warwickshire Regiment adopted 'The Warwickshire Lads', which had been composed by Charles Dibdin in 1769 for the first Shakespeare celebrations at Stratford that year. Other popular tunes of the day were also taken up by regiments such as The Rifle Brigade (formerly the 95th Foot), whose bandmaster, William Miller, adapted the very apt 'I'm Ninety-Five' when in Malta in 1842; The Army Service Corps, which adopted the similarly apt 'Wait for the Wagon' in 1875; and the Royal Horse Guards, which adopted the march from *Aida* after its first performance at Covent Garden in 1876. The popularity of German bandmasters also had much to do with The King's Royal Rifle Corps choosing the 'Huntsman's Chorus' from Weber's opera *Der Freischutz*, although it changed subsequently to Lutzow's 'Wild Hunt'. Much later, **The Parachute Regiment** adopted Wagner's 'The Ride of the Valkyries'. With a humorous touch, the Tank Corps adopted 'My Boy Willie', a Worcestershire folk song, since the first prototype tanks had been christened 'Big Willie' and 'Little Willie' after Kaiser Wilhelm II and his son, Crown Prince Wilhelm of Prussia.

The 35th, later 1st Battalion, The Royal Sussex Regiment, had a French tune, 'Roussillon', as their slow march, a reminder of their defeat of the French Roussillon Regiment before Quebec in 1759. The 14th Foot, later The West Yorkshire Regiment, adopted the French revolutionary march 'Ça Ira' in 1881 in memory of its part in the action at Valenciennes in May 1793. The French were playing the march to inspire their men when Colonel Doyle of the 14th ordered his own drummers to take it up, shouting, 'Come along, my lads. Let's beat the scoundrels to their own damned tune.' Just as music inspired the 14th at Valenciennes, so the sound of the pipes could inspire

Boy drummers of the Seaforth Highlanders in full and service dress, 1909. The drums themselves carry the regimental badge and battle honours.

the Scottish soldier. At Dargai during the Tirah campaign against the Afridis on India's North-west Frontier in October 1897, Piper Findlater of the Gordon Highlanders won the Victoria Cross for continuing to play 'Cock o' the North' to encourage the men despite being hit in both legs. 'Cock o' the North' itself derived from the nickname of the 92nd's founder, the Duke of Gordon. Piper Laidlaw of the 7th (Service) Battalion, The King's Own Scottish Borderers also won the Victoria Cross, playing 'Blue Bonnets over the Border' during a German gas attack on Hill 70 at Loos in September 1915.

Music has also been part of regimental custom. Between about 1866 and the Second World War nightly musical programmes were played in a number of regiments. The 12th Lancers, for example, traditionally played a programme of hymns, possibly linked to the service in Italy in 1794 of part of the regiment, whose officers were presented to Pope Pius VI. In another custom, The Royal Lincolnshire Regiment and The Worcestershire Regiment played each other's regimental marches before their own on ceremonial occasions following their service together at the battle of Sobraon in February 1846 during the First Sikh War; there was a similar practice between the **Royal Marines** and The East Surrey Regiment. The Wiltshire Regiment would play 'Rule Britannia' before its regimental march in band programmes in commemoration of its marine service in the eighteenth century.

Certain marches or tunes also became universally played. Thus, 'The Girl I Left Behind Me', dating from 1758, usually accompanied a regiment leaving a station while 'The Rogue's March', composed about 1727, once accompanied those being 'drummed out' of a regiment for persistent offences. Other tunes became popular at particular periods, such as 'Lillibulero', familiar from its use on the BBC World Service, and which was popular with the army at the time of the Glorious Revolution, when it celebrated the coming of William and Mary to overthrow James II. 'Over the Hills and Far Away' became popular during the early eighteenth century and 'The British Grenadiers', first printed in 1780, in the early nineteenth. 'Cheer, Boys, Cheer' was something of a 'hit' with troops in the Crimean War while 'The Soldiers of the Queen' made the transition from music hall to army in the late nineteenth century. The First World War was marked by a wide variety of songs in the army, such as 'Mademoiselle from Armentières' and, at least for a short time, 'It's a Long Way to Tipperary', composed by Jack Judge, while an example from the Second World War was the German song 'Lilli Marlene', taken up by the British Eighth Army in North Africa.

22. Ceremonies

A number of ceremonies have already been referred to but more should be said of those now most familiar to the public, Trooping the Colour and Beating Retreat. Trooping the Colour is now almost solely linked to the Sovereign's Birthday Parade on Horse Guards Parade in London but in earlier times took place throughout the army. The 1st Battalion, The Sherwood Foresters, for example, always trooped the Colour on Badajoz Day (see chapter 18). Trooping the Colour began as 'Lodging the Colour' in the eighteenth century, certainly being included within the ceremonial of the Foot Guards in 1735. The music played was known as the 'Troop', hence the evolution of the ceremony as 'Trooping the Colour'. The original ceremony took place each night when the Colours were placed for safety in the care of an ensign and carried along the ranks or 'trooped' so that all would know the whereabouts of the night's 'lodging'. In the annual ceremony on Horse Guards Parade, the Colours of the battalion being trooped are initially in the care of non-commissioned officers and other ranks, signifying that they can be trusted to protect them without officers present. The Number One guard on the extreme right of the parade is the escort of the Colours and, since grenadiers were traditionally on the right of the line, the bands play 'The Grenadiers March' during the trooping movements.

Sounding and beating Retreat was also a regular nightly practice from the army's earliest existence in the seventeenth century, being a 'watch setting' at sunset that called the night guard to duty. It then became the custom for the drummers and later the band to play for a half hour before the barrack gates were shut at sunset. Originally, Tattoo, from the Dutch phrase *Doe den tap toe* ('Turn off the taps'), was similar to Retreat, indicating the closure of the taverns and the closing of the gates. However, the two ceremonies appear to have become separated in the late eighteenth century, with Tattoo increasingly becoming a large-scale public entertainment as in the case of the annual Edinburgh Military Tattoo, although Beating Retreat is also a frequent spectacle both in London and the provinces. Before the Second World War Aldershot was renowned for its Grand Searchlight Tattoos. The Royal Tournament, a military display, originated in 1880 as the Grand Military Tournament and Assault at Arms at the Royal Agricultural Hall, Islington, and was originally promoted by the Volunteer Force rather than the army. It was held for the last time in 1999.

A different ceremony was Beating the Credits, when the departure of a regiment from billets in a town was heralded by beat of drum in order to warn householders and merchants who had extended credit to soldiers. Regiments marching through towns with band playing, bayonets fixed and Colours flying were also, and are still, observed on occasions as a sign that a unit has been given the freedom of the city

Massed bands of the Brigade of Guards at Beating Retreat on Horse Guards Parade.

One of the famous inter-war Grand Searchlight Tattoos at Aldershot. Here soldiers re-enact the storming of Rangoon by the 13th, 38th and 41st Foot on 10th May 1824 during the First Burma War.

or town. In the City of London it was long claimed that one of its privileges was to prohibit the passage of troops without the authority of the Lord Mayor. However, a number of regiments were given the privilege at various times including the **Honourable Artillery Company**, the **Grenadier Guards**, The Buffs (Royal East Kent Regiment), The Royal Fusiliers and the **Royal Marines**. Modern regiments maintain their rights to march through 'freedom towns'. Thus, The Duke of Edinburgh's Royal Regiment (Berkshire and Wiltshire) had the freedom of Abingdon, Devizes, Maidenhead, Newbury, Salisbury, Swindon, Wallingford and Windsor while The Devonshire and Dorset Regiment has the freedom of Barnstaple, Blandford, Bridport, Christchurch, Dorchester, Exeter, Lyme Regis, Poole, Torbay and Weymouth.

DRILL DISPLAY - EARL OF BATH'S REGT., 1685

CAPTURE OF NAMUR, 1695

Two scenes from one of the inter-war tattoos at Tidworth, featuring a re-enactment of the capture of Namur on 4th August 1695 during the Nine Years War or War of the League of Augsburg. The Earl of Bath's Regiment became the 10th Foot, later the Royal Lincolnshire Regiment.

23. Uniform and equipment

Uniform plays an important part in moulding the image of an army for both soldiers and civilians alike and in differentiating military and civilian society. On occasions military dress tended to follow civilian fashion, but on others it influenced civilian styles as is shown by the wellington boot, the cardigan and the balaclava.

The first regulations for the army's uniforms were promulgated in 1678, and by 1689 the distinctive red coat of the British infantry had appeared although the lace and facing colours on the uniforms still varied and it was only in 1727 that more effort was made to ensure conformity. The first uniform coats were loose and worn with bandoliers while headgear was a broad-brimmed hat with the sides turned up so that it did not impede drill. Ultimately, the turning up of the sides resulted in the tricorn and the coat was buttoned back to produce lapels and a collar, which enabled the use of facing colours to distinguish between regiments. A remembrance of the original facing colours of regimental dress can be detected in some nicknames. The 4th Foot, later The King's Own Royal Regiment (Lancaster), was thus 'Barrell's Blues' and the 35th Foot, later The Royal Sussex Regiment, were the 'Orange Lilies' because William III had permitted them to adopt orange facings. Two regiments continued to be known by their original facing colour, The Green Howards being so named originally to distinguish them from the 'Buff Howards' – the 3rd Foot, later The Buffs – also commanded by a Colonel Howard at a time when regiments were more generally known by the name of the Colonel.

Lace of different hues also adorned the edges of the turning, the button holes and the side-pocket flaps, originally as additional protection against wear but then as regimental distinctions in themselves. Gaiters were introduced about 1705 to protect breeches and stockings and, with the introduction of the flintlock, the bandolier was replaced by cartridge boxes carried on shoulder belts. The celebrated Brown Bess musket was also introduced about 1740 and remained in service until the 1840s.

Re-enactors at the Festival of History, Kelmarsh, 2006, in the uniform of the 68th Foot Regiment (Durham Light Infantry) as worn towards the latter half of the Napoleonic Wars, in which the regiment served in the Peninsula.

Two illustrations dating from August 1854 of the new French-style tunics and shakos introduced into the army in the following year. The first depicts light infantry and cavalry uniforms, and the second depicts artillery uniforms. As well as an acknowledgement of supposed French military prowess, the new style was also a reaction against the uncomfortable and restricted uniforms worn during the Crimean War.

The grenadier cap was adopted in the early eighteenth century, this and the tricorn only being replaced by the cylindrical leather shako in 1800. In 1808 the practice of wearing the hair in a greased queue also ended although officers of The Royal Welch Fusiliers continued to wear the 'flash', five black silk ribbons at the collar, as a reminder of the queue bag in which the queue was tied. In 1900 all ranks in the regiment were permitted to wear it. Another development of the French Revolutionary and Napoleonic Wars was a shorter tunic or coatee and trousers, which had started as overalls to cover the breeches and leggings.

After the defeat of Napoleon, uniforms reached the height of their sartorial elegance and impracticability, with the long-tailed coat reappearing in 1820 together with much gold lace and ever more elaborate head-dress such as the bell-topped shako and the 2 foot (61 cm) high bearskin with swan's feather adopted in the Household Cavalry, which caused Wellington to be blown off his horse by a sudden gust of wind at a review in 1829. However, the officer's gorget worn at the throat, a reminder of neck armour, was abolished in 1830: the red tabs worn by colonels and above are a reminder of the former gorget fasteners. Partly in tribute to supposed French military prowess and partly in response to public criticism of tight uniforms, high stocks and restricting equipment straps, looser French-style tunics were adopted after the Crimean War, the army having also replaced the percussion musket, first introduced in 1839, with the Enfield rifled musket in 1853. The smaller, French tapered shako also became standard, but the double-breasted tunic of 1855 quickly gave way to a single-breasted tunic in 1856.

Borrowing martial styles from other armies was very common in Europe and North America. Thus, with the unexpected defeat of the French by the Prussians in 1870-1, a Prussian-style spiked helmet replaced the shako between 1878 and 1881 although The Highland Light Infantry and The Cameronians retained the earlier French-style shako. The Prussian use of the breech-loading Dreyse 'needle-gun' also encouraged the introduction of the Snider conversion of the Enfield rifle in 1866, to be replaced by the Martini-Henry in 1874. With territorialisation in 1881 facings were standardised, with blue for 'Royal' regiments, white for English line infantry, yellow for Scots and green for Irish regiments. However, in one case a dress distinction was preserved since the 'valise star' worn by the 29th Foot, from at least the early eighteenth century on their pouches and after 1871 on the more comfortable valise equipment, was carried over into The Worcestershire Regiment.

Service in the colonies had often resulted in experimentation and in adaptation to uniform. Indeed, this had been true of service in North America in the eighteenth century when small skull caps and cut-down jackets were adopted and blankets were carried in bandolier fashion. In the first half of the nineteenth century it was common to wear forage caps and shell jackets on campaign as in the First China War (1839-42) and the First Maori War (1846-7) in New Zealand. From about 1846 onwards Indian troops began to wear earth-coloured clothing, the first being Harry Lumsden's Corps of Guides, and the British regiments in India similarly adopted what became known as *khaki* – the Hindustani word for dust being *khak* – by dyeing their hot-weather white uniforms with substances such as tea, mud, coffee, curry powder, tobacco and mulberry juice. The first to have done so appears to have been the 52nd Foot, later 2nd Battalion, The Oxfordshire and Buckinghamshire Light Infantry, during the Indian Mutiny in 1857 followed by the 61st, later 2nd Battalion, The Gloucestershire Regiment. In 1873 Sir Garnet (later Field Marshal Lord) Wolseley had his expeditionary force in the Ashanti War wear grey serge. However, regiments sent on campaign from Britain still primarily wore red serge campaign dress, but red proved too good a target for marksmen with modern magazine rifles, as in the First Boer War (1880-1). As a result, the last battle to be fought in the red coat was Ginniss on the Egyptian-Sudanese frontier in December 1885. The British themselves adopted the Lee Metford bolt-action magazine rifle in 1888, to be followed by the Lee Enfield in 1896, a weapon that, like the Brown Bess, was to enjoy long and valuable service, in this case into the 1960s. Khaki service dress then came in for all foreign service in 1897 and for all at home in 1902.

The full dress was never restored after the First World War and was mostly confined to regimental bands, with the exception of Household troops. In 1936 a new blue serge ceremonial uniform was introduced as No 1 Dress but, entirely understandably, was never popular.

A speculative illustration of a new khaki service dress proposed for the British army in 1884. However, khaki service dress was not introduced for all foreign service until 1897 and for field service at home until 1902.

24. Battles and campaigns

The battle honours borne on the Colours have increasingly been only a selection of those won by regiments because after 1922 regiments were directed to carry no more than twenty-five honours on the Colours, of which up to ten could be for the First World War. In 1956 a similar limitation was placed on battle honours for the Second World War. With the amalgamations after 1958, it was ruled that up to forty honours could be carried on each of the Sovereign's and Regimental Colours. The first battle honour was awarded to the 15th Light Dragoons, later 15th The King's Hussars, for the action at Emsdorff in July 1760. Thereafter, each major war and campaign has generated them although battle honours were often awarded long after the event, those for Marlborough's victories in the War of Spanish Succession, for example, being granted only in 1882.

Some battle honours are unique to particular regiments. The Royal Dublin Fusiliers, for example, by virtue of the 102nd and 103rd being originally European regiments of the East India Company in Madras and Bombay respectively, had fifteen honours that were granted to no others, such as 'Beni Boo Ali' (March 1821), 'Condore' (December 1758) and 'Kirkee' (November 1817). 'Deig' (November 1804) was

A postcard dating from between 1908 and 1914 and showing the badge and selected battle honours of the Oxfordshire and Buckinghamshire Light Infantry, ranging from Quebec (1759) to the South African War (1899-1902).

awarded only to The Royal Munster Fusiliers, the 101st and 104th being originally both Bengal European regiments, and 'Wilhelmstahl' (June 1762) was awarded only to The Royal Northumberland Fusiliers. The Royal Scots alone had 'Nagpore' (December 1817) while only The Royal Berkshire Regiment had 'Tofrek' (March 1885), the Berkshires also receiving their 'Royal' title for this desperate action against the dervishes outside Suakin on the Red Sea coast of the Sudan. Collectively, Tofrek, Tamai (March 1884), in which dervishes broke temporarily into the British square, and Abu Klea (January 1885) during Wolseley's abortive expedition to save Gordon at Khartoum, where another square was temporarily breached, inspired Sir Henry Newbolt's celebrated poem *Vitae Lampada,* with the lines 'Play up! play up! and play the game!'. 'Nile, 1884-5; Abu Klea' was awarded to The Royal Sussex Regiment and the 19th Hussars but Tamai was subsumed within the more general honour 'Egypt 1884'. 'Defence of Kimberley' (October 1899 to February 1900) was a battle honour unique to The Loyal North Lancashire Regiment, Kimberley being the third town, with Ladysmith and Mafeking, besieged by the Boers at the start of the South African War.

Many regiments carried honours for major battles. 'Malplaquet' (September 1709) was the most common honour for the War of Spanish Succession, being borne by twenty-two regiments, while the most common honour for the Peninsular War was 'Vittoria' (June 1813), borne by forty-nine regiments. 'Waterloo' (June 1815) was borne by thirty-eight regiments while the most common honour for the Crimean War was the 'soldier's battle' fought in the fog at Inkerman (November 1854). The more general campaign honours could be borne by even more, such as 'South Africa 1899-1902', borne by sixty-three regiments.

Particular actions were also kept as regimental anniversaries, although not always with quite the same ceremony as some of those already mentioned such as Badajoz Day and Minden Day. Other such regimental anniversaries include those of Almanza (27th April 1707), kept in both **The Royal Anglian Regiment**, deriving from The Royal Norfolk Regiment, and **2nd Battalion, the Yorkshire Regiment (Green Howards)**; Bligny (6th June 1918), kept in The Shropshire Light Infantry; Guadaloupe (10th June 1759), kept in **1st Battalion, the Duke of Lancaster's Regiment (King's, Lancashire and Border)** and deriving originally from The Manchester Regiment; Nunshigum (13th April 1944), kept in **The Royal Scots Dragoon Guards** and deriving from the 3rd Carabiniers; Sahagun (21st December 1808), kept in the 15th/19th The King's Royal Hussars; and Wagon Hill (6th January 1900), kept in **1st Battalion, The Rifles** and originating with The Devonshire Regiment.

Wearing the uniform of the 47th Foot during the American War of Independence, re-enactors at the Festival of History, 2006. The 47th became part of the Loyal North Lancashire Regiment, which alone had the battle honour 'Defence of Kimberley' from the South African War.

25. Medals

Battles and campaigns are also recalled by the medals awarded to soldiers although this did not become common practice until the mid nineteenth century. The orders of chivalry such as the Order of the Garter (1344) and the Order of the Bath (1399) were originally martial honours, and distinguished officers continued to be honoured by new orders created in the nineteenth century such as the Order of St Michael and St George (1818), the Order of the Star of India (1861) and the Royal Victorian Order (1896) as well as by a substantial increase in the number of military awards within the Order of the Bath after 1725. Some senior officers also received the first campaign medals such as some struck for the siege of Gibraltar (1779-83) and the Maida Medal for a successful action against the French in southern Italy in July 1806. Senior officers also received the Army Gold Medal (1810) and the Army Gold Cross (1813) for battles during the Peninsular War. However, ordinary soldiers were not so honoured. A few medals were awarded to ordinary soldiers during the English Civil War such as the 'Forlorn Hope' Medal instituted by Charles I, and some men as well as some officers received Cromwell's Dunbar Medal (1650). However, it was the East India Company that first issued medals to its troops, including King's regiments present, for the First Maratha War (1778-82), the Second Mysore War (1780-3), the siege of Seringapatam (1799) and the expedition to Egypt (1801).

The East India Company continued to issue its own medals while privately commissioned medals were common in the yeomanry and volunteer units of the French Revolutionary and Napoleonic Wars. However, King's troops were not always permitted to wear the East India Company's medals, and the first campaign medal to be authorised for all officers and men in the British Army was the Waterloo Medal issued in 1816. Inscribed bars, or clasps, were added to the ribbon of a campaign medal for an individual battle or action within the campaign. The Military General Service Medal covering the campaigns between 1793 and 1814 was not issued until 1847 and then only for those still surviving. A total of twenty-nine clasps were available for different actions, two soldiers each qualifying for fifteen of them, Corporal James Talbot of the 45th Foot, later 1st Battalion, The Sherwood Foresters, and Private Daniel Loochstadt of the 60th, later The King's Royal Rifle Corps. The British government's own general service medal for Indian campaigns between 1799 and 1826, the Army of India Medal, with twenty-one clasps, was awarded to survivors only in 1851.

The Crimea Medal (1854) was the first after the Waterloo Medal to be issued promptly. Thereafter, the issue of medals was, rightly, nearly automatic. With the sheer numbers involved in the First World

The Waterloo Medal, the first campaign medal awarded to both officers and men. Designed by Thomas Wyon, it was also the first medal to have the recipient's name engraved around the edge, using a machine newly invented by Thomas Jerome and Charles Harrison at the Royal Mint.

Left: *The three general medals of the First World War, collectively known as 'Pip, Squeak and Wilfred'; (from left to right) the 1914-15 Star, the Victory Medal 1914-18 and the British War Medal 1914-18.*

Right: *The 1939-45 War Medal (left) and the Defence Medal (right).*

War, only three general medals were issued – the 1914 Star or 1914-15 Star, the War Medal and the Victory Medal – the three together being universally known as 'Pip, Squeak and Wilfred'. They were at least still individually identified with the soldier's name and regiment. By contrast, the eight Stars and two medals (Defence Medal and War Medal) awarded for the Second World War were not individually named and, in the case of the Stars, were issued in a copper zinc alloy, which unnecessarily

The 1939-45 Star (left) and the Burma Star (right).

Captured Russian guns and bells from Sebastopol after their arrival at Woolwich Arsenal in February 1856. Victoria Crosses continue to be cut from the bronze of such a captured Russian gun.

further cheapened the whole exercise.

Beyond campaign medals, there are individual gallantry awards. The supreme decoration for gallantry is the Victoria Cross, which was instituted at the Queen's initiative on 29th January 1856 and which is still made from the bronze of Russian cannon captured during the Crimean War. Originally, it carried with it an annual annuity of £10, raised to £50 in 1898 for those in distressed circumstances following the poverty into which Piper Findlater of the Gordons fell after being discharged as a result of his wounds at Dargai. In 1959 the annuity was raised to £100. The first awards were gazetted in February 1857 and backdated to the beginning of the Crimean War. The first man to win the VC was a naval officer, Mate (later Rear-Admiral) Charles Lucas, who won it for throwing a live Russian shell off HMS *Hecla* during

Queen Victoria presenting the first Victoria Crosses in Hyde Park in June 1857. Sixty-two individuals received their awards on that occasion.

The medals of Major-General Sir John Edmund Gough, who won his VC in Somaliland in April 1903. Both his father and uncle also had won the VC, during the Indian Mutiny. The other medals are the CMG, Central Africa Medal, Queen's Sudan Medal, Queen's South Africa Medal, King's South Africa Medal, Africa General Service Medal, 1914 Star, British War Medal, Victory Medal, and Khedive's Sudan Medal. Gough's KCB is not shown.

the Allied bombardment of Bomarsund in the Baltic on 21st June 1854. The first six awards to soldiers were all for the battle of the Alma on 20th September 1854, four going to the Scots Fusilier Guards, later the **Scots Guards**, and two to the 23rd Foot, later The Royal Welch Fusiliers. Between 1856 and 1914 soldiers won 348 of the 522 VCs awarded.

There have been three cases of both fathers and sons winning the VC. Field Marshal Lord Roberts won it while serving with the Bengal Artillery during the Indian Mutiny, and his son, Lieutenant Freddy Roberts, The King's Royal Rifle Corps, as related earlier, won his posthumously at Colenso. Another of the Colenso VCs was Captain (later General Sir) Walter Congreve of The Rifle Brigade, whose son, Brevet-Major 'Billy' Congreve, also of the Rifle Brigade, won his posthumously in July 1916. General Sir Charles Gough of the Bengal European Cavalry and his brother, Sir Hugh Gough, both won the VC in the Mutiny while Sir Charles's son, 'Johnnie'

The grave of Private Frederick Hitch, VC, in the churchyard of Chiswick parish church in west London. A member of the 12/24th Foot (later the South Wales Borderers), Hitch won one of eleven VCs awarded for the action at Rorke's Drift on 22nd and 23rd January 1879.

A set of miniatures, as worn with mess dress, of an officer of the 99th (Royal Bucks Yeomanry) Field Regiment, Royal Artillery: (from left to right): the CBE, the 1939-45 Star, the Burma Star, the Defence Medal, the 1939-45 War Medal, the Coronation Medal (Queen Elizabeth II) and the Territorial Decoration. (Courtesy of the Bucks Military Museum Trust)

Gough of The Rifle Brigade, won his in Somaliland in April 1903, later being killed by a German sniper in February 1915 when chief of staff to Sir Douglas Haig. Three pairs of brothers have won the VC.

In both the Crimean War and the Indian Mutiny quite large numbers of VCs were awarded so that, in the inaugural ceremony in Hyde Park in June 1857, Queen Victoria bestowed them on no less than sixty-two individuals. The eleven VCs won at Rorke's Drift in January 1879 remain the largest number awarded to a single regiment in one engagement while six were won 'before breakfast' by the 1st Battalion, The Lancashire Fusiliers when it landed on W Beach at Cape Helles on the Gallipoli peninsula on 25th April 1915. Another nine VCs were won on the same day at V Beach. The most for a single engagement were the twenty-one awarded for the Battle of Inkerman on 5th November 1854, although this was a confusing battle over a considerable expanse and some have argued that the twenty won for the assault on the Redan, part of the defences of Sebastopol, on 18th June 1855 should more rightly be considered the most for a single action. Another twelve were won when the Redan was stormed again on 8th September 1855 while a total of twenty-one VCs were awarded during the Indian Mutiny for the operations of the first relief of Lucknow between 24th and 27th September 1857 and thirty for the second relief of Lucknow between 12th and 16th November 1857, of which seventeen were won in storming the Sikandar Bagh on 16th November. The regiment that has won most VCs is the 24th Foot, later The South Wales Borderers, with twenty-two awards, reflecting not only Isandlwana and Rorke's Drift but also, for example, five won for saving lives in a storm at sea off the Andaman Islands in May 1867. Only one other VC has been awarded for bravery not in the face of the enemy, this being for Private Timothy O'Hara of The Rifle Brigade for putting out a fire in a railway car full of ammunition in June 1866 during the campaign to contain the Fenian incursions into Canada. The last VCs to be awarded were for the Falklands campaign in 1982, Sergeant Ian McKay of the 3rd Battalion, The Parachute Regiment winning it posthumously at Mount Longdon on 12th June and Lieutenant Colonel 'H' Jones of the regiment's 2nd Battalion, also posthumously, at Goose Green on 28th May.

The Distinguished Service Order (DSO) for officers of field rank (major and above) specially recommended in despatches for distinguished field service was instituted in 1886, and the Military Cross (MC) for commissioned officers of and below the

The medals of a Great War soldier of the Bucks Battalion, Territorial Force, who served in the Special Constabulary during the Second World War: (from left to right) the 1914-15 Star, the Victory Medal, the War Medal, the Territorial Medal, the Special Constabulary Medal and the Defence Medal (1939-45). (Courtesy of the Bucks Military Museum Trust)

rank of captain and to warrant officers was instituted in December 1914, followed by the Military Medal (MM) for non-commissioned officers and men in April 1916. The Distinguished Conduct Medal (DCM), which is the equivalent to the MC for warrant officers and non-commissioned ranks, is much older than the latter, having been instituted in 1854. Soldiers could also be mentioned in despatches at the conclusion of a campaign or battle but, prior to 1843, only officers were so mentioned. The George Cross, instituted in September 1940, may also be won by soldiers for acts of gallantry not in direct face of the enemy.

Long service awards include the Meritorious Service Medal (MSM), instituted in 1846 for sergeants and warrant officers who had distinguished themselves other than in battle; the Long Conduct and Good Service Medal, instituted in 1833 for soldiers who had completed eighteen years' service; and the Territorial Decoration (TD), which replaced the earlier Volunteer Decoration (VD).

The memorial on the battlefield of Sedgemoor near Bridgwater, Somerset. Sedgemoor, in which the army of James II defeated the Duke of Monmouth's rebel forces on 6th July 1685, was the first and last battle fought by the British standing army on English soil.

26. Monuments, memorials and military sites

The British have taken little interest in the preservation of their battlefields compared to other countries, and it was only in 1994 that a limited degree of protection was afforded by English Heritage's Battlefields Register, itself prompted in part by major road construction across the battlefield of Naseby (June 1645), at which the New Model Army defeated the last major field army at the disposal of Charles I. Encouraged by the success of organisations in the United States such as the Association for the Preservation of Civil War Sites (APCWS), there is now a Battlefields Trust in Britain dedicated to saving British battlefields. Indeed, its first major venture is to assist in the purchase of the site of Langport (July 1645), where the last Royalist army in the west was defeated. Most battles on British soil predate the establishment of a standing army although one of the few to have adequate visitor facilities is Culloden (April 1746), where the Duke of Cumberland destroyed the Jacobite army of 'Bonnie Prince Charlie'. More common is a simple memorial near the centre of the field, as at Sedgemoor (July 1685), effectively the first and last battle fought by the British standing army on English soil, although there were skirmishes during the advance of the Jacobite army as far south as Derby in 1745.

Consequently, battlefields on which British troops have fought tend to be overseas, and some are especially well preserved. This is particularly true of those in Canada and, in the case of the United States, those dating from the American War of Independence and the Anglo-American War of 1812-14, when British forces seized

The Old North Bridge, Concord, Massachusetts, where two British soldiers were buried in 1775.

Washington and burned the presidential mansion – hence its later name of The White House, following repainting to hide the scorch marks. By the North Bridge at Concord in Massachusetts, for example, are buried two unknown British soldiers killed in the exchange of fire with American militiamen on 19th April 1775. The American War of Independence was the only major war that the British have lost and, significantly, it is one for which no battle honours were granted, with the exception of the seizure of St Lucia in the West Indies in 1778 and the naval battle of the Saints off Martinique in 1782. Among many preserved former British military installations, Canada has Fort York in Toronto and the United States has Forts Niagara, William Henry, Ticonderoga and Crown Point within New York state alone.

The battlefields of the Zulu War and the two Anglo-Boer Wars (1880-1 and 1899-1902) are still reasonably well preserved, the white-washed cairns of Isandlwana having a particular poignancy. Battlefield tours are increasingly popular, and even the Crimean peninsula has now been opened to touring groups. The most accessible battlefields are those of the two world wars in Europe and, especially, those of the First World War.

It was also the First World War that brought the large-scale commemoration of British war dead. There were monuments and memorials in Britain before 1914 but, most often, these were for officers such as those found in many cathedrals and churches and in larger cemeteries such as Kensal Green in London. Wellington's memorial opposite his former London home, Apsley House, at Hyde Park Corner

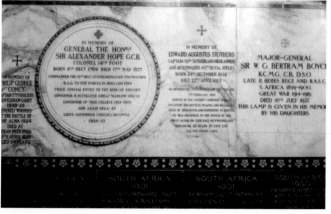

Some of the memorials to officers in the chapel of the Royal Military Academy, Sandhurst.

features statues of soldiers in Napoleonic uniform including a trooper of the Household Cavalry, a Guardsman and a Highlander of the Black Watch. One of Wellington's cavalry generals, later Marquess of Londonderry, is remembered by a magnificent equestrian statue of him in full hussar uniform in Durham. A later example is the obelisk to Lieutenant Thomson of the 17th Lancers, killed at Balaclava, at Hatherleigh in Devon.

Mass graves had been the fate of most ordinary soldiers in the eighteenth and early nineteenth centuries, and the bones from many European battlefields, including Waterloo, were swept up in the 1820s for importation through Hull to be turned into fertiliser by Yorkshire bone-grinding companies. Some early war monuments appeared in Germany in the 1820s and 1830s, but the obelisk in the Royal Hospital Gardens at Chelsea erected in 1853 is very unusual for this early period in Britain in listing the names of all 255 officers and men of the 24th Foot, later The South Wales

Above: *The obelisk in the Royal Hospital Gardens at Chelsea commemorating the officers and men of the 24th Foot killed at Chillianwallah during the First Sikh War.*

The memorial chapel of the Staffordshire Regiment in Lichfield Cathedral has a screen with a series of Zulu shields and assegais, the 80th Foot (later the 2nd Battalion of the regiment) having served in the Zulu War of 1879.

Above left: *The Cenotaph in Whitehall, here seen decorated with Remembrance Sunday wreaths, was unveiled on 11th November 1920. It was designed by Sir Edwin Lutyens. The word derives from the Greek for 'empty tomb'.*

Above right: *The village war memorial at Mullion on the Lizard peninsula in Cornwall lists the units as well as the names of the fallen of the First World War.*

Borderers, killed at Chillianwallah in January 1849. Another later example is the massive lion erected in Forbury Gardens in Reading, commemorating the men of the 66th Foot (2nd Battalion, The Royal Berkshire Regiment) lost at Maiwand in 1881. Thereafter, it was not until the South African War of 1899-1902 that monuments of this kind became more usual, such as that on Coombe Hill near Wendover in Buckinghamshire, which was unveiled in 1904 and which records the names of 148 men from the county killed in South Africa. Other South African War memorials feature statues of soldiers in service dress, such as that at Slade Park at Headington in Oxford, commemorating The Oxfordshire Light Infantry, or in full dress as in the memorial to The Lancashire Fusiliers at Bury. It was a large-scale war in the context of other conflicts involving Britain since the end of the Napoleonic Wars in 1815 but nothing like the scale of the conflict between 1914 and 1918.

The Great War, as it was popularly known (the same term had once been used for the conflict between 1793 and 1815), necessitated the introduction of conscription in 1916 and cost Britain some 673,000 military dead. As elsewhere, the war resulted in much more elaborate collective commemoration. The Imperial War Museum, for example, was a wartime creation in 1917 while Armistice Day was marked for

The Guards Memorial opposite Horse Guards Parade in London. The wreaths are in the form of the regimental badges of the five Guards regiments.

The war memorial of the Royal Artillery at Hyde Park Corner includes a massive First World War howitzer and a statue of an artillery driver. He is depicted in wet weather gear, with a metal guard on his leg to prevent it being crushed between his two horses.

the first time on 11th November 1919, the suggestion originating with a former British High Commissioner to South Africa, Sir Percy Fitzpatrick. In November 1920 the Cenotaph was unveiled in Whitehall and an unknown soldier interred in the Tomb of the Unknown Warrior in Westminster Abbey, an idea suggested by the Reverend David Railton, MC. Armistice Day then became a favoured day for the unveiling of the town and village war memorials that listed each community's dead. Usually, such town and village memorials, to which the names of those lost in the Second World War were added in due course, are simple lists of the dead. Occasionally, however, men's regiments are listed, as at Mullion in Cornwall. Many are either crosses or representations of the Cenotaph. Others, however, incorporate statues of soldiers of the First World War, such as that at Helston in Cornwall, or those in London commemorating The Royal Fusiliers at Holborn Bars, High Holborn, the **Royal Artillery** at Hyde Park Corner and the Guards opposite Horse Guards Parade. By contrast, the memorial to The King's Regiment in Liverpool incorporates statues of soldiers in both seventeenth- and eighteenth-century uniform.

In some places there were also memorial halls or other buildings such as the War Memorial Hospital at Deal in Kent. A more unusual memorial in Leith Rosebank Cemetery is to the 214 officers and men of the 1/7th Battalion, The Royal Scots, who were killed in a train crash in May 1915, while in St Albans in Hertfordshire are to be found street memorials. War memorials were also erected by schools and colleges and by commercial companies: an example of the latter is to be found in Liberty's in Regent Street, London. A more unusual memorial is the Sandham Memorial Chapel at Burghclere in Hampshire, decorated between 1926 and 1932 with Stanley Spencer's paintings of service in Mesopotamia. Within Edinburgh Castle there is the Scottish National War Memorial, opened in 1927 and depicting in its stained glass and bronzes all types of war service and including transport mules, carrier pigeons and even the mice and canaries used to detect gas attacks.

To some extent, initially, Armistice Day was also a day of celebration by some ex-servicemen, but this was criticised, and in November 1927 the former annual Victory Ball in the Albert Hall became the annual Festival of Remembrance. Pilgrimages to the battlefields also began in the 1920s as the Imperial (later Commonwealth) War Graves Commission completed their beautifully maintained cemeteries, each adorned with a Stone of Remembrance and Cross of Sacrifice. There were also memorials to

The Thiepval Memorial by Sir Edwin Lutyens carries the names of over 70,000 dead whose graves are unknown. This is the principal memorial to those lost on the Somme in 1916.

those with no known grave such as the Menin Gate, unveiled at Ypres in July 1927, and then carrying 54,896 names, and the Thiepval Memorial unveiled on the Somme in August 1932 and then carrying 73,412 names. The 'Silent Cities', as Kipling called the cemeteries, were to be found wherever British troops had fought and died. Similar cemeteries of the Second World War can be found from Dunkirk in France to El Alamein in Egypt and Kohima in Burma, where the memorial to the British 2nd Division, echoing that erected for the Spartans at Thermopylae, proclaims: 'When you go home, tell them of us and say, For your tomorrow we gave our today.'

Away from the commemoration of the dead, reminders of the military past are to be found in buildings. While most castles predate the standing army, those near the coast, such as Dover in Kent or Pendennis at Falmouth in Cornwall (itself one of Henry VIII's coastal works), were often incorporated into later coastal defence works and, as such, were garrisoned by regulars. The continuing threat of invasion led to other coastal defence works. Remaining defences from the Napoleonic Wars include the Redoubt at Eastbourne, Fort Amherst at Chatham, the Harwich Redoubt and the martello towers, of which twenty-five remain although many have been converted to other uses. The distinctive circular shape and the name both derive from the extraordinary resilience of such a fortification on Mortella Point, Corsica, when bombarded by HMS *Fortitude* and HMS *Juno* in 1794. The three most accessible towers are those at Eastbourne, Folkestone and Dymchurch. With the revival of invasion fears in the 1850s, the so-called Palmerston fortifications were erected around naval ports such as Portsmouth and Plymouth. Many of these mid-Victorian works are now open to the public, including Forts Nelson, Widley and Brockhurst among the Portsmouth defences, Nothe Fort at Weymouth (part of the Portland defences), where there is a museum of coastal defence, and the Needles Battery on the Isle of Wight. Fort Nelson houses the artillery collection of the Royal Armouries. Second World War pillboxes have also frequently survived, although they are often in poor condition or inaccessible.

There are also many reminders of the military past in barracks such as those at Berwick-upon-Tweed, Fort George in Scotland or Dorchester, where the Dorset Military Museum is housed in the former keep of the regimental depot, in army

Some of the badges carved in the chalk at Fovant in Wiltshire by soldiers stationed on Salisbury Plain during the First World War. That at second left is of the Australian Imperial Force.

camps such as Aldershot and in the grounds of the former Royal Victoria Military Hospital at Netley, most of which was demolished in 1966. Sometimes, the reminder of the past can be unusual. At Fovant near Salisbury, for example, First World War soldiers carved twelve regimental badges into the chalk hillside including those of The Wiltshire Regiment, The London Rifle Brigade and The Royal Warwickshire Regiment: all are preserved by the Fovant Badges Society.

The chapel of the Royal Victoria Military Hospital at Netley, Hampshire.

27. Family traditions

As a result of two world wars, military service became part of the history of many families in Britain in the twentieth century. The advent of cheap mass photography at the beginning of the century has also bequeathed to many families fading snaps – often in the form of postcards – of khaki-clad ancestors. Occasionally, too, there are letters or even diaries. Officer ancestors are relatively easy to trace through the basic source of the published Army Lists, dating from about 1702 although not produced regularly until 1754. Moreover, the records for officers kept in the War Office papers at the Public Record Office (PRO) at Kew are far more complete than for ordinary soldiers. There are, for example, a series of records of officers' services.

For the ordinary soldier, at least the name of the regiment is required since most War Office records are arranged by regiment. At the PRO Class WO97 has soldiers' attestation and discharge papers for the period between 1760 and 1913, but there are also regimental description books (WO25) and pay lists and muster rolls (WO12 *et al*) as well as files on deserters and pension payments. A medal may often be an entrée to a family tradition, and there are medal rolls (WO100 *et al*) that may yield a soldier's number and regiment if this is not already known. The PRO has opened some of the surviving personnel files of soldiers (WO364), with more being filmed for release (WO363), and those of officers (WO339 and 374) who served in the army during the First World War, although many were lost to enemy action during the Blitz. Service records after 1920 are still closed and are retained by the Army Records Office at Hayes.

A demobilisation certificate transferring a wartime soldier of the Royal Army Service Corps to the Army Reserve in March 1919. Frederick Butler, a pre-war jockey, had undertaken remount duties during the Great War.

The PRO also holds a range of records relating to the auxiliary forces although these are more likely to be found in local county record offices. Indeed, the ballot lists and muster rolls of the militia between 1757 and 1831 are the closest records to a national census available because, although the census began in 1801, enumerators' schedules are not available before 1841. Equally valuable in this regard are the surviving compilations under the provisions of the *posse comitatus* and the Defence of the Realm Act of 1798 as well as those for the two Defence Acts in 1803. Since militia families became a charge on the parish during embodied militia service, much information is also to be found in papers relating to the maintenance of these families. Most records of the auxiliary forces will be found in lieutenancy collections or those of families connected to the lieutenancy. The PRO does have correspondence (HO50) and pay lists (WO13) for the auxiliaries generally during the Revolutionary and Napoleonic Wars. Militia records do exist for earlier periods, principally in PRO classes E36, E101 and the *Calendars of State Papers Domestic,* but they rarely have personal information. Some militia records after 1852 are to be found in PRO WO68 but, where they do exist, most Victorian records are to be found in the county record offices. The same is true of the Territorials, Volunteer Training Corps and Home Guard although the PRO holds the attestation forms for the Imperial Yeomanry of the South African War (WO128). Home Guard attestation forms are still held by the Army Medal Office at Droitwich and are not available to the public.

Some records relating to service in India can also be found in the British Library's Oriental and India Office collections. Archives are also retained by the National Army Museum and, for the twentieth century, by the Imperial War Museum. Indeed, the National Army Museum holds surviving regimental records for the disbanded Irish regiments and the **9th/12th Royal Lancers**. Though a few regimental registers of births, marriages and deaths can be found at the PRO, most are retained by the Office of Population Censuses and Surveys' Family Records Centre, formerly at St Catherine's House and now in Myddelton Street, London EC1.

This can only provide a brief glimpse of the means available for tracing military ancestry, and those interested are referred to the guides listed in the bibliography.

Appendix I:
Regimental and military museums

Note: While the regimental and other museums are open to the public, visiting hours may be restricted and, indeed, appointments may be necessary. It is advisable, therefore, to check in advance.

Aberdeen
The Gordon Highlanders Museum, St Luke's, Viewfield Road, Aberdeen AB15 7XH. Telephone: 01224 311200. Website: www.gordonhighlanders.com

Aldershot
Aldershot Military Museum, Woodstock Annexe, Queen's Avenue, Aldershot GU11 2LG. Telephone: 01252 314598. Website: www.hants.gov.uk/museum/aldershot
Army Medical Service Museum, Keogh Barracks, Ash Vale, Aldershot GU12 5RQ. Telephone: 01252 340320. Website: www.army.mod.uk/medical/ams_museum
Army Physical Training Corps Museum, Queen's Avenue, Aldershot GU11 2LB. Telephone: 01252 347168. Website: www.army.mod.uk/aptc/museum
Parachute Regiment and Airborne Forces Museum, Browning Barracks, Aldershot GU11 2BU. Telephone: 01252 349619. Website: www.army.mod.uk/para/af-museum

Alloway by Ayr
Ayrshire Yeomanry Museum, Rozelle House, Monument Road, Alloway by Ayr, Ayrshire KA7 4NQ. Telephone: 01292 445447. Website: www.south-ayrshire.gov.uk/galleries/rozellehouse.htm

Alnwick
The Royal Northumberland Fusiliers Museum, The Abbot's Tower, Alnwick Castle, Alnwick, Northumberland NE66 1NG. Telephone: 01665 602152. Website: www.northumberlandfusiliers.org.uk

Arborfield
The REME Museum of Technology, Isaac Newton Road, Arborfield, Berkshire RG2 9NJ. Telephone: 0118 976 3375. Website: www.rememuseum.org.uk

Armagh
The Royal Irish Fusiliers Museum, Sovereign's House, The Mall, Armagh, County Armagh, Northern Ireland BT61 9DL. Telephone: 028 3752 2911. Website: www.rirfus-museum.freeserve.co.uk

Ashton-under-Lyne
The Museum of the Manchesters, Town Hall, Market Place, Ashton-under-Lyne, Lancashire OL6 6DL. Telephone: 0161 342 2254. Website: www.tameside.gov.uk/museumsandgalleries

Ayr
Ayrshire Yeomanry Museum, Rozelle House Galleries, Monument Road, Ayr KA7 4NQ. Telephone: 01292 442065.

Ballymena
Museum of The Royal Irish Regiment, St Patrick Barracks, Ballymena, County Antrim BT43 7NX. Telephone: 028 2566 1383. Website: www.army.mod.uk/royalirish (Please telephone to make an appointment before visiting.)

Barnsley
13th/18th Royal Hussars, Cannon Hall Museum, Cawthorne, Barnsley, SouthYorkshire S75 4AT. Telephone: 01226 790270. Website: www.lightdragoons.org.uk/regimental_history/museums.php

Barnstaple
The Royal Devon Yeomanry, Museum of Barnstaple and North Devon, The Square, Barnstaple, Devon EX32 8LN. Telephone: 01271 346747. Website: www.devonmuseums.net

Bedford
The Bedfordshire Yeomanry Collection, Bedford Museum, Castle Lane, Bedford MK40 3XD. Telephone: 01234 353323. Website: www.bedfordmuseum.org

Belfast
The Royal Ulster Rifles Regimental Museum. Enquiries to Regimental Headquarters, The Royal Irish Regiment, 5 Waring Street, Belfast BT1 2EW. Telephone: 028 9023 2086. Website: www.geocities.com/rurmuseum

Berwick-upon-Tweed
Museum of the King's Own Scottish Borderers, The Barracks, The Parade, Berwick-upon-Tweed, Northumberland TD15 1DG. Telephone: 01289 307426 or 332817. Website: www.kosb.co.uk

Blackburn
Blackburn Museum and Art Gallery, Museum Street, Blackburn, Lancashire BB1 7AJ. Telephone: 01254 667130. Website: www.blackburn.gov.uk [East Lancashire Regiment.]

Blair Atholl
Museum of the Atholl Highlanders, Blair Castle, Blair Atholl, Pitlochry, Perthshire PH18 5TL. Telephone: 01796 481207. Website: www.blair-castle.co.uk (A privately raised regiment)

Blandford Forum
Royal Signals Museum, Blandford Camp, Blandford Forum, Dorset DT11 8RH. Telephone: 01258 482248. Website: www.army.mod.uk/royalsignalsmuseum

The Old Gaol in Buckingham houses the Buckinghamshire Military Museum.

Bodmin
The Duke of Cornwall's Light Infantry Regimental Museum, The Keep, Bodmin, Cornwall PL31 1EG. Telephone: 01208 72810. Website: www.lightinfantry.org.uk/regiments/dcli/duke_index.htm

Bovington
The Tank Museum, Bovington, Dorset BH20 6JG. Telephone: 01929 405096. Website: www.tankmuseum.co.uk

Brading
Aylmer Military Collection, Nunwell House, Coach Lane, Brading, Isle of Wight PO36 0JQ. Telephone: 01983 407240. [Home Guard.]

Brecon
The South Wales Borderers and Monmouthshire Regimental Museum, The Barracks, Brecon, Powys LD3 7EB. Telephone: 01874 613310. Website: www.rrw.org.uk

Buckingham
Buckinghamshire Military Museum, The Old Gaol Museum, Market Hill, Buckingham, Buckinghamshire MK18 1JX. Telephone: 01280 823020. [Auxiliary forces.]

Bury
The Fusiliers Museum Lancashire, Wellington Barracks, Bolton Road, Bury, Lancashire BL8 2PL. Telephone: 0161 764 2208. Website: www.fusiliersmuseum-lancashire.org.uk

Bury St Edmunds
The Suffolk Regiment Museum, The Keep, Gibraltar Barracks, Newmarket Road, Bury St Edmunds, Suffolk IP33 3RN. Telephone: 01284 752394. Website: www.suffolkregiment.org/Museum.html

Caernarfon
The Royal Welch Fusiliers Regimental Museum, The Castle, Caernarfon LL55 2AY. Telephone: 01286 673362. Website: www.rwfmuseum.org.uk

Camberley
The Royal Logistic Corps Museum, Princess Royal Barracks, Deepcut, Camberley, Surrey GU16 6RW. Telephone: 01252 833371. Website: www.royalpioneercorps.co.uk/rpc/history_museum.htm
The Royal Military Academy (Sandhurst Collection), Sandhurst, Camberley, Surrey GU15 4PQ. Telephone: 01276 63344. Website: www.sandhurst.mod.uk

Canterbury
The Buffs (Royal East Kent Regiment) Museum, Royal Museum and Art Gallery, 18 High Street, Canterbury, Kent CT1 2RA. Telephone: 01227 452747. Website: www.canterbury.co.uk

The King's Own Royal Border Regiment has its headquarters and its museum at Carlisle Castle.

Dorchester Keep, the former barracks, now a museum of the Devon and Dorset regiments.

Cardiff
1st The Queen's Dragoon Guards Regimental Museum, Cardiff Castle, Cardiff CF10 2RB. Telephone: 029 2078 1213 (Castle) or 029 2078 1232 (Dragoon Guards). Website: www.qdg.org.uk (Closed for redevelopment until November 2007)
The Welch Regiment (41st Foot) Museum, Black and Barbican Towers, Cardiff Castle, Cardiff CF1 2RB. Telephone: 029 2022 9367. Website: www.rrw.org.uk

Carlisle
The Border Regiment and King's Own Royal Border Regiment Museum, Queen Mary's Tower, The Castle, Carlisle, Cumbria CA3 8UR. Telephone: 01228 532774. Website: www.kingsownbordermuseum.btik.com

Carmarthen
Carmarthenshire County Museum, Abergwili, Carmarthen SA31 2JG. Telephone: 01267 228696. Website: www.carmarthenshire.gov.uk [Auxiliary forces.]

Chelmsford
The Essex Regiment Museum, Oaklands Park, Moulsham Street, Chelmsford, Essex CM2 9AQ. Telephone: 01245 605700. Website: www.chelmsford.gov.uk

Chester
Cheshire Military Museum, The Castle, Chester CH1 2DN. Telephone: 01244 327617. Website: www.chester.ac.uk/militarymuseum [22nd (Cheshire) Regiment, 3rd Carabiniers (Prince of Wales's Dragoon Guards).]

Chicksands
The Military Intelligence Museum, Chicksands, Shefford, Bedfordshire SG17 5PR. Telephone: 01462 752896. Website: www.army.mod.uk/intelligencecorps

Coldstream
The Coldstream Museum, 12 Market Square, Coldstream, Berwickshire TD12 4BD. Telephone: 01890 882630. Website: www.holy-island.info/coldstream-museum

Colne
British in India Museum, Newtown Street, Colne, Lancashire BB8 0JJ. Telephone: 01282 613129. Website: www.lancashire.gov.uk

Cupar
The Fife and Forfar Yeomanry Collection, Yeomanry House, Castlebank Road, Cupar, Fife KY15 4BL. Telephone: 01334 656155. Website: www.armymuseums.org.uk (By appointment only)

Derby
Regimental Museum of 9th/12th Royal Lancers (Prince of Wales) and Derbyshire Yeomanry Collection, Derby Museum and Art Gallery, The Strand, Derby DE1 1BS. Telephone: 01332 716659. Website: www.derby.gov.uk/LeisureCulture/MuseumsGalleries

Doncaster
The King's Own Yorkshire Light Infantry Regimental Gallery, Doncaster Museum and Art Gallery, Chequer Road, Doncaster, South Yorkshire DN1 2AE. Telephone: 01302 734293. Website: www.doncaster.gov.uk

Dorchester
The Keep Military Museum, The Keep, Bridport Road, Dorchester, Dorset DT1 1RN. Telephone: 01305 264066. Website: www.keepmilitarymuseum.org

Dover
The Princess of Wales's Royal Regiment and Queen's Regiment Museum, Dover Castle, Dover, Kent CT16 1HU. Telephone: 01304 240121. Website: army.mod.uk/pwrr

Durham
The Durham Light Infantry Museum, Aykley Heads, Durham DH1 5TU. Telephone: 0191 384 2214. Website: www.durham.gov.uk

Duxford
The Royal Anglian Regiment Museum and Cambridgeshire Regimental Collection, Imperial War Museum, Duxford, Cambridge CB2 4QR. Telephone: 01223 835000. Website: www.royalanglianmuseum.org.uk

Eastbourne
The Royal Sussex Regiment Museum and the Queen's Royal Irish Hussars Museum, Sussex Combined Services Museum, The Redoubt, Royal Parade, Eastbourne, East Sussex BN22 7AQ. Telephone: 01323 410300. Website: www.eastbournemuseums.co.uk

Edinburgh
The Royal Scots Dragoon Guards (Carabiniers and Greys) Museum, The Castle, Edinburgh EH1 2YT. Telephone: 0131 310 5102. Website: www.army.mod.uk/scotsdg

Fort Nelson at Fareham, Hampshire, has the artillery collection of the Royal Armouries.

The Royal Scots Regimental Museum, The Castle, Edinburgh EH1 2YT. Telephone: 0131 310 5018. Website: www.theroyalscots.co.uk

The Scottish National War Memorial, The Castle, Edinburgh EH1 2YT. Telephone: 0131 226 7393. Website: www.snwm.org

National War Museum, The Castle, Edinburgh EH1 2NG. Telephone: 0131 247 4413. Website: www.nms.ac.uk

Enniskillen

The Royal Inniskilling Fusiliers Regimental Museum, The Castle, Enniskillen, County Fermanagh, Northern Ireland BT74 7HL. Telephone: 028 6632 3142. Website: www. inniskilling.com

Fareham

Royal Armouries Fort Nelson, Fort Nelson, Portsdown Hill Road, Fareham, Hampshire PO17 6AN. Telephone: 01329 233734. Website: www.armouries.org.uk

The Royal Military Police Museum, The Defence College of Policing and Guarding, Postal Point 38, Southwick Park, Fareham, Hampshire PO17 6EJ. Telephone: 023 9228 4897. Website: www.army.mod.uk/rmp

Gateshead

101 Northumbrian Fd Regt RA (V) Museum, Napier Armoury, Alexandra Road, Gateshead, Tyne and Wear NE8 4HX. Telephone: 0191 239 6132. Website: www.armymuseums. co.uk (By appointment only)

Gillingham

The Royal Engineers Museum, Prince Arthur Road, Gillingham, Kent ME4 4UG. Telephone: 01634 822839. Website: www.remuseum.org.uk

Glasgow

The Regimental Museum of the Royal Highland Fusiliers, 518 Sauchiehall Street, Glasgow G2 3LW. Telephone: 0141 332 5639. Website: www.rhf.org.uk

Gloucester

Soldiers of Gloucestershire Museum, Gloucester Docks, Gloucester GL1 2HE. Telephone: 01452 522682. Website: www.glosters.org.uk

Grantham

The Queen's Royal Lancers Regimental Museum, Belvoir Castle, Grantham, Lincolnshire NG32 1PD. Telephone: 0115 957 3295. Website: www.qrl.uk.com

Guernsey

Royal Guernsey Militia Museum, Castle Cornet, St Peter Port, Guernsey, Channel Islands. Telephone: 01481 706963. Website: www.museum.guernsey.net (Currently closed for refurbishment)

Guildford

The Queen's Royal Surrey Regiment Museum, Clandon House, Clandon Park, West Clandon, Guildford, Surrey GU4 7RQ. Telephone: 01483 223419. Website: www.queensroyalsurreys.org.uk

Halifax

The Duke of Wellington's Regimental Museum, Bankfield Museum, Akroyd Park, Boothtown Road, Halifax, West Yorkshire HX3 6HG. Telephone: 01422 352334 or 354823. Website: www.dwr.org.uk

Hamilton

The Cameronians (Scottish Rifles), Low Parks Museum, 129 Muir Street, Hamilton ML3 6BJ. Telephone: 01698 328232. Website: www.cameronians.org

Hereford

Herefordshire Light Infantry Museum, TA Centre, Harold Street, Hereford HR1 2QX. Telephone: 01432 359917. Website: www.armymuseums.org.uk (By appointment only)

Hever

The Kent and Sharpshooters Yeomanry Regimental Museum Trust, Hever Castle, Hever, Edenbridge, Kent TN8 7NG. Telephone: 01732 865224. Website: www.heverCastle. co.uk or www.kysmuseum.org.uk

Hitchin

The Hertfordshire Yeomanry and Artillery Museum, Hitchin Museum and Art Gallery, Paynes Park, Hitchin, Hertfordshire SG5 1EQ. Telephone: 01462 434476. Website: www.north-herts.gov.uk

Hull

4th Battalion East Yorkshire Regimental Collection, Ferens Art Gallery, Queen Victoria Square, Hull, East Yorkshire HU1 3DX. Telephone: 01482 300300. Website: www. hullcc.gov.uk/museums

Huntingdon

Cromwell Museum, Grammar School Walk, Huntingdon, Cambridgeshire PE29 3LF. Telephone: 01480 375830. Website: www.cambridgeshire.gov.uk/cromwell

Inverness

The Highlanders Museum (Queen's Own Highlanders Collection), Fort George, Ardersier, Inverness IV1 2TD. Telephone: 01667 462800. Website: www.army.mod.uk/highlanders/ museums.htm

Lancaster

The King's Own Royal Regiment Museum, Lancaster City Museum, Market Square, Lancaster LA1 1HT. Telephone: 01524 64637. Website: www.kingsownmuseum.plus.com

Leeds

The Royal Armouries Museum, Armouries Drive, Leeds, West Yorkshire LS10 1LT Telephone: 0113 220 1916. Website: www.royalarmouries.org

Leicester

The Royal Leicestershire Regimental Gallery, New Walk Museum and Art Gallery, 53 New Walk, Leicester LE1 7EA. Telephone: 0116 225 4900. Website: www.leicestermuseums. ac.uk

Lichfield

The Staffordshire Regiment Museum, Whittington Barracks, Lichfield, Staffordshire WS14 9PY. Telephone: 01543 434394.
Website: www.staffordshireregimentmuseum.com

Lincoln

The Lincolnshire Regiment Collection, Museum of Lincolnshire Life, Old Barracks, Burton Road, Lincoln LN1 3LY. Telephone: 01522 528448.
Website: www.lincolnshire.gov.uk/museumoflincolnshirelife

Liverpool

The Liverpool Scottish Regimental Museum, Forbes House, Botanic Road, Liverpool. Telephone: 07952 169285. Website: www.liverpoolscottish.org.uk (By appointment only)

London

Bank of England Museum, Threadneedle Street, London EC2R 8AH. Telephone: 020 7601 5491. Closed weekends. Website: www.bankofengland.co.uk [Bank Volunteers]
Firepower, The Royal Artillery Museum, Royal Arsenal, Woolwich, London SE18 6ST. Telephone: 020 8855 7755. Website: www.firepower.org.uk
The Guards Museum, Wellington Barracks, Birdcage Walk, London SW1A 6HQ. Telephone: 020 7414 3271. Website: www.theguardsmuseum.com
The Honourable Artillery Company Museum, Armoury House, City Road, London EC1Y 2BQ. Telephone: 020 7382 1537. Website: www.hac.org.uk (By appointment only)
Imperial War Museum, Lambeth Road, London SE1 6HZ. Telephone: 020 7416 5320. Website: www.iwm.org.uk

Inns of Court and City Yeomanry Museum, 10 Stone Buildings, Lincoln's Inn, London WC2A 3TG. Telephone: 020 7405 8112.

The London Irish Rifles Regimental Museum, Flodden Road, Camberwell, London SE5 9LL. Telephone: 020 7820 4040. Website: www.londonirishrifles.com (By appointment only)

London Regiment Volunteers Museum, 213 Balham High Road, Balham, London SW17 7BQ. Telephone: 020 8672 1168.

The London Scottish Regimental Museum, 95 Horseferry Road, London SW1P 2DX. Telephone: 020 7630 1639. Website: www.londonscottishregt.org (By appointment only)

National Army Museum, Royal Hospital Road, Chelsea, London SW3 4HT. Telephone: 020 7730 0717. Website: national-army-museum.ac.uk

The Royal Fusiliers Museum, HM Tower of London, Tower Hill, London EC3N 4AB. Telephone: 0870 756 6060. Website: www.army.mod.uk/fusiliers/museums.htm or www.hrp.org.uk/tower

The Royal Hospital Museum, Royal Hospital Road, Chelsea, London SW3 4SR. Telephone: 020 7881 5200. Website: www.chelsea-pensioners.co.uk

Wellington Museum, Apsley House, 149 Piccadilly, London W1V 9FA. Telephone: 020 7499 5676. Website: www.english-heritage.org.uk

Westminster Dragoons Museum, 87 Fulham High Street, London SW6 3JS. Telephone: 020 7384 4201. Website: www.westminsterdragoons.co.uk

Loughborough

The Leicestershire Yeomanry Collection, Loughborough War Memorial Museum, Carillon Tower, Queen's Park, Granby Street, Loughborough, Leicestershire LE11 2EW. Telephone: 01509 263370. Website: www.irmf.org.uk

Luton

Bedfordshire and Hertfordshire Regimental Association Museum, Museum and Art Gallery, Wardown Park, Luton, Bedfordshire LU2 7HA. Telephone: 01582 546722. Website: www.luton.gov.uk/museums

Maidstone

The Queen's Own Royal West Kent Regimental Museum, Maidstone Museum and Art Gallery, St Faith's Street, Maidstone, Kent ME14 1LH. Telephone: 01622 602838. Website: www.museum.maidstone.gov.uk

Middle Wallop

Museum of Army Flying, Middle Wallop, Stockbridge, Hampshire SO20 8DY. Telephone: 01264 784421. Website: www.flying–museum.org.uk

Milton Keynes

Bletchley Park Trust, The Mansion, Bletchley Park, Bletchley, Milton Keynes, Buckinghamshire MK3 6EB. Telephone: 01908 640404. Website: www.bletchleypark.org.uk (Cryptology Centre in Second World War.)

Monmouth

Castle and Regimental Museum, The Castle, Monmouth NP25 3BS. Telephone: 01600 772175. Website: www.monmouthcastlemuseum.org.uk [Royal Monmouth Royal Engineers (Militia).]

Newcastle upon Tyne

15th/19th The King's Royal Hussars and Northumberland Hussars Yeomanry, A Soldier's Life Gallery, Discovery Museum, Blandford Square, Newcastle upon Tyne NE1 4JA. Telephone: 0191 232 6789. Website: www.twmuseums.org.uk

Newhaven

Newhaven Fort, Newhaven, East Sussex BN9 9DL. Telephone: 01273 517622. Website: www.newhavenfort.org.uk

Newtownards

The Somme Heritage Centre, Whitespots Country Park, 233 Bangor Road, Newtownards, Northern Ireland BT23 7PH. Telephone: 01247 823202. Website: www.irishsoldier.org

Northampton

The Northamptonshire Regiment and Northamptonshire Yeomanry, Abington Park Museum, Park Avenue South, Northampton NN1 5LW. Telephone: 01604 838110. Website: www. northampton.gov.uk/museums

Norwich

The Royal Norfolk Regimental Museum, Shirehall, Market Avenue, Norwich, Norfolk NR1 3JQ. Telephone: 01603 493649. Website: www.rnrm.org.uk or www.museums.norfolk. gov.uk

Nottingham

South Nottinghamshire Hussars Museum, The TA Centre, Hucknall Lane, Bulwell, Nottingham NG6 6AQ. Telephone: 0115 927 2251. Website: www.armymuseums.org.uk
The Castle Museum and Art Gallery, off Maid Marian Way, Nottingham NG1 6EL. Telephone: 0115 915 3700. Website: www.nottinghamcity.gov.uk [Sherwood Foresters.]

Oakham

Volunteer Soldier Gallery, Rutland County Museum, Catmose Street, Oakham, Rutland LE15 6HW. Telephone: 01572 758440. Website: www.rutland.gov.uk/museum or www. lrmf.org.uk [Auxiliary forces.]

Oxford

Regimental Museum of Oxfordshire and Buckinghamshire Light Infantry, Slade Park TA Barracks, Headington, Oxford OX3 7JL. Telephone: 01865 780128. Website: www. armymuseums.org.uk (By appointment only)

Penrith

The Westmorland and Cumberland Yeomanry Museum, Dalemain Historic House and Garden, near Penrith, Cumbria CA11 0HB. Telephone: 01768 486450. Website: www. dalemain.com

Perth

The Black Watch Museum, Balhousie Castle, Hay Street, Perth PH1 5HR. Telephone: 0131 310 8530. Website: www.theblackwatch.co.uk

The Black Watch Museum in Perth.

The Wardrobe in the Cathedral Close at Salisbury is home to The Royal Gloucestershire, Berkshire and Wiltshire Regiment Museum.

Plas Newydd

Ryan Collection (Militaria) and Waterloo Museum, Plas Newydd, Llanfairpwll, Anglesey, North Wales LL61 6DQ. Telephone: 01248 714795. Website: www.nationaltrust.org.uk (Collection relating to Marquess of Anglesey at Waterloo Museum.)

Preston

Museum of Lancashire, Stanley Street, Preston, Lancashire PR1 4YP. Telephone: 01772 534075. Website: www.lancashire.gov.uk/education/museums [14/20th King's Hussars; Duke of Lancaster's Own Yeomanry.]

The Loyal North Lancashire Regiment Museum, Regimental Headquarters, The Queen's Lancashire Regiment, Fulwood Barracks, Preston, Lancashire PR2 8AA. Telephone: 01772 260584. Website: www.army.mod.uk/qlr

Richmond

The Green Howards Regimental Museum, Trinity Church Square, Richmond, North Yorkshire DL10 4QN. Website: www.greenhowards.org.uk

Rotherham

The York and Lancaster Regimental Museum, Central Library and Art Centre, Walker Place, Rotherham, South Yorkshire S65 1JH. Telephone: 01709 336633. Website: www.rotherham.gov.uk

Salisbury

The Royal Gloucestershire, Berkshire and Wiltshire Regiment Museum, The Wardrobe, 58 The Close, Salisbury, Wiltshire SP1 2EX. Telephone: 01722 419419. Website: www.thewardrobe.org.uk

Shrewsbury

The Shropshire Regimental Museum, Shrewsbury Castle, Castle Street, Shrewsbury, Shropshire SY1 2AT. Telephone: 01743 358516. Website: www.discovershropshire.org.uk [King's Shropshire Light Infantry.]

Southsea

The Royal Marines Museum, Eastney Barracks, Southsea, Portsmouth, Hampshire PO4 9PX. Telephone: 023 9281 9385. Website: www.royalmarinesmuseum.co.uk

The D Day Museum, Clarence Esplanade, Southsea, Portsmouth, Hampshire PO5 3NT. Telephone: 023 9282 7261. Website: www.ddaymuseum.co.uk

Stafford
Museum of the Staffordshire Yeomanry (Queen's Own Royal Regiment), The Ancient High House, Greengate Street, Stafford ST16 2JA. Telephone: 01785 619131. Website: www.armymuseums.org.uk

Stirling
The Argyll and Sutherland Highlanders Regimental Museum, The Castle, Stirling FK8 1EH. Telephone: 01786 475165. Website: www.argylls.co.uk

Stratfield Saye
Wellington Exhibition, Stratfield Saye House, Stratfield Saye Park, near Reading RG7 2BZ. Telephone: 01256 882882. Website: www.stratfield-saye.co.uk

Swindon
The Royal Wiltshire Yeomanry Museum, c/o A (Royal Wiltshire Yeomanry) Squadron, Yeomanry House, Church Place, Swindon, Wiltshire SN1 5EH. Telephone: 01793 523865. Website: www.armymuseums.org.uk

Taunton
Somerset Military Museum, Taunton Castle, Castle Green, Taunton, Somerset TA1 4AA. Telephone: 01823 320201. Website: www.sommilmuseum.org.uk [Somerset Light Infantry.]

Twickenham
The Royal Military School of Music Museum, Kneller Hall, Twickenham, Middlesex TW2 7DU. Telephone: 020 8898 5533. Website: www.army.mod.uk/music/kneller_hall (By appointment only)

Warminster
The Infantry and Small Arms School Corps Weapons Collection, HQ SASC, Land Warfare Centre, Warminster, Wiltshire BA12 0DJ. Telephone: 01985 222487. Website: www.army.mod.uk/sasc (By appointment only)

Warwick
The Queen's Own Hussars Museum, The Lord Leycester Hospital, 60 High Street, Warwick CV34 4BH. Telephone: 01926 492035. Website: www.qohmuseum.org.uk
The Royal Warwickshire Regiment Museum, St John's House, Warwick CV34 4NF. Telephone: 01926 491653. Website: www.warwickfusiliers.co.uk
The Warwickshire Yeomanry Museum, The Court House, Jury Street, Warwick CV34 4EW. Telephone: 01926 492212 (tourist information centre). Website: www.warwick-uk.co.uk

Westerham
Wolfe Museum, Quebec House (NT), Westerham, Kent TN16 1TD. Telephone: 01732 868381. Website: www.nationaltrust.org.uk

Weymouth
Nothe Fort Museum of Coastal Defence, Barrack Road, Weymouth, Dorset DT4 8UF. Telephone: 01305 766626. Website: www.fortressweymouth.co.uk

Winchester
The Gurkha Museum, Peninsula Barracks, Romsey Road, Winchester, Hampshire SO23 8TS. Telephone: 01962 842832. Website: www.thegurkhamuseum.co.uk
The Light Infantry Museum, Peninsula Barracks, Romsey Road, Winchester, Hampshire SO23 8TS. Telephone: 01962 828550. Website: www.winchestermilitarymuseums.co.uk
The Royal Green Jackets Museum, Peninsula Barracks, Romsey Road, Winchester, Hampshire SO23 8TS. Telephone: 01962 828528. Website: www.royalgreenjackets.co.uk
The Royal Hampshire Regiment Museum and Memorial Garden, Serle's House, Southgate Street, Winchester, Hampshire SO23 9EG. Telephone: 01962 863658. Website: www.royalhampshireregimentmuseum.co.uk

Part of the complex of Peninsula Barracks at Winchester, where there are four separate regimental museums: those of the Gurkhas, The Light Infantry, Horse Power (The King's Royal Hussars) and The Royal Green Jackets.

Horse Power, The King's Royal Hussars Museum in Winchester, The King's Royal Hussars, Peninsula Barracks, Romsey Road, Winchester, Hampshire SO23 8TS. Telephone: 01962 828539. Website: www.krh.org.uk

Windsor
The Household Cavalry Museum, Combermere Barracks, Windsor, Berkshire SL4 4DP. Telephone: 01753 755194. Website: www.householdcavalry.co.uk
The Royal Berkshire Yeomanry Cavalry Museum, The TA Centre, Bolton Road, Windsor, Berkshire SL4 3JG. Telephone: 01753 860600. Website: www.army.mod.uk/royalsignals/94sigsqn.htm (Please write for an appointment.)

Worcester
Museums of the Worcestershire Regiment and Yeomanry Cavalry, Worcester City Museum and Art Gallery, Foregate Street, Worcester WR1 1DT. Telephone: 01905 25371. Website: www.worcestercitymuseums.org.uk
The Commandery Civil War Centre, Sidbury, Worcester WR1 2HU Telephone: 01905 361821. Website: www.worcestercitymuseums.org.uk (Currently closed for redevelopment)

York
The Prince of Wales's Own Regiment of Yorkshire and The Royal Dragoon Guards Regimental Museums, 3 Tower Street, York YO1 9SB. Telephone: 01904 662790 or 642036. Website: www.rdgmuseum.org.uk or www.armymuseums.org.uk
The Kohima Museum, Imphal Barracks, Fulford Road, York YO10 4AU. Telephone: 01904 665086. Website: www.armymuseums.org.uk [2nd Division.] (By appointment only)
Queen's Own Yorkshire Yeomanry Museum, Yeomanry Barracks, Fulford Road, York YO10 4ES. Telephone: 01904 620320 or 01482 881974 for information on the collections. Website: www.armymuseums.org.uk (By appointment only)

Appendix II:
Regimental lineage

(This is an abbreviated lineage, giving the most significant titles of existing regiments, the dates in parentheses representing that of formation.)

The **Household Cavalry Regiment** and the **Household Cavalry Mounted Regiment** (1992) comprises:

1. **The Life Guards** (1661).

2. **The Blues and Royals** (Royal Horse Guards and 1st Dragoons) (1969), from the Royal Horse Guards (1661) and The Royal Dragoons (1st Dragoons) (1661).

The **Royal Armoured Corps** comprises:

1. **1st The Queen's Dragoon Guards** (1959), from 1st King's Dragoon Guards (1685) and The Queen's Bays (2nd Dragoon Guards) (1685).

2. **The Royal Scots Dragoon Guards (Carabiniers and Greys)** (1971), from 3rd Carabiniers (Prince of Wales's Dragoon Guards) (1922) and The Royal Scots Greys (2nd Dragoons) (1681). 3rd Carabiniers (Prince of Wales's Dragoon Guards) from 3rd Dragoon Guards (Prince of Wales's) (1685) and 6th Dragoon Guards (Carabiniers) (1685).

3. **The Royal Dragoon Guards** (1992), from 4/7th Royal Dragoon Guards (1922) and 5th Royal Inniskilling Dragoon Guards (1922). 4/7th Royal Dragoon Guards from 4th Royal Irish Dragoons (1685) and 7th Dragoon Guards (Princess Royal's) (1688). 5th Royal Inniskilling Dragoon Guards from 5th Dragoon Guards (Princess Charlotte of Wales's) (1685) and The Inniskillings (6th Dragoons) (1689).

4. **The Queen's Royal Hussars (The Queen's Own and Royal Irish)** (1993), from The Queen's Own Hussars (1958) and The Queen's Royal Irish Hussars (1958). The Queen's Own Hussars from 3rd The King's Own Hussars (1685) and 7th Queen's Own Hussars (1689). The Queen's Own Royal Irish Hussars from 4th Queen's Own Hussars (1685) and 8th King's Royal Irish Hussars (1693).

5. **9th/12th Royal Lancers (Prince of Wales's)** (1960), from 9th Queen's Royal Lancers (1715) and 12th Royal Lancers (Prince of Wales's) (1715).

6. **The King's Royal Hussars** (1992), from The Royal Hussars (Prince of Wales's Own) (1969) and 14th/20th King's Hussars (1922). Royal Hussars from 10th Royal Hussars (Prince of Wales's Own) (1715) and 11th Hussars (Prince Albert's Own) (1715). 14th/20th from 14th King's Hussars (1715) and 20th Hussars (1862).

7. **The Light Dragoons** (1992), from 13th/18th Royal Hussars (Queen Mary's Own) (1922) and 15th/19th The King's Hussars (1922). 13/18th from 13th Hussars (1715) and 18th Royal Hussars (Queen Mary's Own) (1858). 15/19th from 15th The King's Hussars (1759) and 19th Royal Hussars (Queen Alexandra's Own) (1858).

8. **The Queen's Royal Lancers** (1993), from 16th/5th The Queen's Royal Lancers (1922) and 17/21st Lancers (1922). 16th/5th from 16th The Queen's Lancers (1759) and 5th Royal Irish Lancers (1689). 17th/21st from 17th Lancers (Duke of Cambridge's Own) (1759) and 21st Lancers (Empress of India's) (1858).

The Royal Tank Regiment (1917).

The Royal Regiment of Artillery (1716).

Corps of Royal Engineers (1717).

Royal Corps of Signals (1920).

The Guards Division comprises:

1. **Grenadier Guards** (1656).

2. **Coldstream Guards** (1650).

3. **Scots Guards** (1660).

4. **Irish Guards** (1900).

5. **Welsh Guards** (1915).

The Scottish Division comprises:

The Royal Regiment of Scotland (2006) from The Royal Scots (The Royal Regiment) (1633), The Royal Highland Fusiliers (Princess Margaret's Own Glasgow and Ayrshire Regiment) (1959), The King's Own Scottish Borderers (1881), The Black Watch (Royal Highland Regiment) (1881), The Highlanders (Seaforth, Gordons and Camerons) (1994), and The Argyll and Sutherland Highlanders (Princess Louise's) (1881). The Royal Scots, formerly 1st Foot (1633). The Royal Highland Fusiliers (Princess Margaret's Own Glasgow and Ayrshire Regiment) from The Royal Scots Fusiliers (1881), formerly 21st Foot (1678), and The Highland Light Infantry (City of Glasgow Regiment) (1881), from 71st Foot (1777) and 74th Foot (1787). The King's Own Scottish Borderers, formerly 25th Foot (1689). The Black Watch (Royal Highland Regiment) (1881), from The Black Watch, formerly 42nd Foot (1739), and 73rd Foot or Perthshire Regiment (1780). The Highlanders (1994) from Queen's Own Highlanders (Seaforth and Camerons) (1961) and The Gordon Highlanders (1881). Queen's Own Highlanders from Seaforth Highlanders (Ross-shire Buffs, The Duke of Albany's) (1881), formerly 72nd Foot (1777) and 78th Foot (1793), and The Queen's Own Cameron Highlanders (1881), formerly 79th Foot (1793). The Gordon Highlanders from 75th Foot (1787) and 92nd Foot (1793). The Argyll and Sutherland Highlanders (Princess Louise's) (1881) from 91st Foot (1794) and 93rd Foot (1799).

The Queen's Division comprises:

1. **The Princess of Wales's Royal Regiment (Queen's and Royal Hampshires)** (1992) from The Queen's Regiment (1966) and The Royal Hampshire Regiment (1881). The Queen's from The Queen's Royal Surrey Regiment (1959). The Queen's Own Buffs, The Royal Kent Regiment (1961), The Royal Sussex Regiment (1881) and The Middlesex Regiment (Duke of Cambridge's Own) (1881). The Queen's Royal Surrey Regiment from The Queen's Royal Regiment (West Surrey) (1881), formerly 2nd Foot (1661), and The East Surrey Regiment (1881), from 31st Foot (1702) and 70th Foot (1758). The Queen's Own Buffs from The Buffs (Royal East Kent Regiment) (1881), formerly 3rd Foot (1665) and The Queen's Own Royal West Kent Regiment (1881), from 50th Foot (1755) and 97th Foot (1824). Royal Sussex from 35th Foot (1701) and 107th Foot (1853). Middlesex from 57th Foot (1755) and 77th (1787). Royal Hampshires from 37th Foot (1702) and 67th Foot (1756).

2. **The Royal Regiment of Fusiliers** (1968) from The Royal Northumberland Fusiliers (1881), formerly 5th Foot (1674), The Royal Warwickshire Fusiliers (1963), formerly The Royal Warwickshire Regiment (1881) and 6th Foot (1673), The Royal Fusiliers (City of London Regiment), formerly 7th Foot (1685), and The Lancashire Fusiliers (1881), formerly 20th Foot (1688).

3. **The Royal Anglian Regiment** (1964) from 1st East Anglian Regiment (Royal Norfolk and Suffolk) (1959), 2nd East Anglian Regiment (Duchess of Gloucester's Own Royal Lincolnshire and Northamptonshire) (1960), 3rd East Anglian Regiment (16th/44th Foot) (1958), and The Royal Leicestershire Regiment (1881), formerly 17th Foot (1688). 1st East Anglian from The Royal Norfolk Regiment (1881), formerly 9th Foot (1685), and The Suffolk Regiment (1881), formerly 12th Foot (1685). 2nd East Anglian from The Royal Lincolnshire Regiment (1881), formerly 10th Foot (1685), and The Northamptonshire Regiment (1881), from 48th Foot (1741) and 58th Foot (1755). 3rd East Anglian from The Bedfordshire and Hertfordshire Regiment (1881), formerly 16th Foot (1688), and The Essex Regiment (1881), from 44th Foot (1741) and 56th Foot (1757).

The King's Division comprises:

1. **The Duke of Lancaster's Regiment (King's, Lancashire and Border)** (2006) from The King's Own Royal Border Regiment (1959), The King's Regiment (1959) and The Queen's Lancashire Regiment (1970). The King's Own Royal Border Regiment (1959) from The King's Own Royal Regiment (Lancaster) (1881), formerly 4th Foot (1680), and The Border Regiment (1881), from 34th Foot (1702) and 55th Foot (1755). The King's Regiment (1959) from The King's Regiment (Liverpool) (1881), formerly 8th Foot (1685), and The Manchester Regiment (1881), from 63rd Foot (1757) and 96th Foot (1824). The Queen's Lancashire Regiment (1970) from The Lancashire Regiment (Prince of Wales's Volunteers) (1958) and The Loyal Regiment (North Lancashire) (1881), from 47th Foot (1741) and 81st Foot (1793). The Lancashire Regiment from The East Lancashire Regiment (1881) and The South Lancashire Regiment (Prince of Wales's Volunteers) (1881). The East Lancashire Regiment from 30th Foot (1702) and 59th Foot (1755). The South Lancashire Regiment from 40th Foot (1717) and 82nd Foot (1793).

2. **The Yorkshire Regiment (14th/15th, 19th and 33rd/76th Foot)** (2006) from The Prince of Wales's Own Regiment of Yorkshire (1958), The Green Howards (Alexandra, Princess of Wales's Own Yorkshire Regiment) (1688), and The Duke of Wellington's Regiment (1881). The Prince of Wales's Own Regiment of Yorkshire (1958) from The West Yorkshire Regiment (The Prince of Wales's Own) (1881), formerly 14th Foot (1685), and The East Yorkshire Regiment (Duke of York's Own) (1881), formerly 15th Foot (1685). The Green Howards (Alexandra, Princess of Wales's Own Yorkshire Regiment), formerly 19th Foot (1688). The Duke of Wellington's Regiment (West Riding) (1881) from 33rd Foot (1702) and 76th Foot (1787).

The Prince of Wales's Division comprises:

1. **The Mercian Regiment** (2007) from The Cheshire Regiment (1881), The Worcestershire and Sherwood Foresters Regiment (29th/45th Foot) (1970), and The Staffordshire Regiment (The Prince of Wales's) (1959). The Cheshire Regiment (1881), formerly 22nd Foot (1689). The Worcestershire and Sherwood Foresters Regiment (29th/45th Foot) (1970) from The Worcestershire Regiment (1881) and The Sherwood Foresters (Nottinghamshire and Derbyshire Regiment) (1881). The Worcestershire Regiment from 29th Foot (1694) and 36th Foot (1701). The Sherwood Foresters from 45th Foot (1741) and 95th Foot (1823). The Staffordshire Regiment (The Prince of Wales's) (1959) from The South Staffordshire Regiment (1881) and The North Staffordshire Regiment (The Prince of Wales's) (1881). The South Staffordshire Regiment from 38th Foot (1705) and 80th Foot (1793). The North Staffordshire Regiment from 64th Foot (1756) and 98th Foot (1824).

2. **The Royal Welsh** (2006) from The Royal Welch Fusiliers (1921) and The Royal Regiment of Wales (24th/41st Foot) (1969). The Royal Welch Fusiliers (1921), formerly The Royal Welsh Fusiliers (1881) and 23rd Foot (1689). The Royal Regiment of Wales (24th/41st Foot) (1969) from The South Wales Borderers (1881), formerly 24th Foot (1689), and The Welch Regiment (1921), formerly The Welsh Regiment (1881), from 41st Foot (1719) and 69th Foot (1758).

The Royal Irish Division comprises:

The Royal Irish Regiment (27th (Inniskilling), 83rd, 87th and UDR) (1992) from The Royal Irish Rangers (27th) (Inniskilling), 83rd and 87th) (1968) and The Ulster Defence Regiment (1970). The Royal Irish Rangers from The Royal Inniskilling Fusiliers (1881), The Royal Ulster Rifles (1921), formerly The Royal Irish Rifles (1881), and The Royal Irish Fusiliers (Princess Victoria's). Royal Inniskillings from 27th Foot (1689) and 108th Foot (1854). The Royal Irish Rifles from 83rd Foot (1793) and 86th Foot (1793). The Royal Irish Fusiliers from 87th Foot (1793) and 89th Foot (1793).

The Light Division comprises:

1. **The Rifles** (2007) from The Devonshire and Dorset Light Infantry (2005), The Royal Gloucestershire, Berkshire and Wiltshire Light Infantry (2005), The Light Infantry (1968), and The Royal Green Jackets (1966). The Devonshire and Dorset Light Infantry (2005), formerly The Devonshire and Dorset Regiment (1958). The Devonshire and Dorset Regiment from The Devonshire Regiment (1881), formerly 11th Foot (1685), and The Dorset Regiment (1881), from 39th Foot (1702) and 54th Foot (1755). The Royal Gloucestershire, Berkshire and Wiltshire Light Infantry (2005), formerly The Royal Gloucestershire, Berkshire and Wiltshire Regiment (1994). The Royal Gloucestershire, Berkshire and Wiltshire Regiment (1994) from The Gloucestershire Regiment (1881) and The Duke of Edinburgh's Royal Regiment (Berkshire and Wiltshire) (1959). The Gloucestershire Regiment from 28th Foot (1694) and 61st Foot (1756). The Duke of Edinburgh's Royal Regiment from The Royal Berkshire Regiment (Princess Charlotte of Wales's) (1881) and The Wiltshire Regiment (Duke of Edinburgh's) (1881). The Royal Berkshire Regiment from 49th Foot (1743) and 66th Foot (1756). The Wiltshire Regiment from 62nd Foot (1756) and 99th Foot (1824). The Light Infantry (1968) from The Somerset and Cornwall Light Infantry (1959), The King's Own Yorkshire Light Infantry (1881), The King's Shropshire Light Infantry (1881), and The Durham Light Infantry (1881). The Somerset and Cornwall Light Infantry from The Somerset Light Infantry (Prince Albert's) (1881), formerly 13th Foot (1685), and The Duke of Cornwall's Light Infantry (1881) from 32nd Foot (1702) and 46th Foot (1741). The King's Own Yorkshire Light Infantry from 51st Foot (1755) and 105th Foot (1839). The King's Shropshire Light Infantry from 53rd Foot (1755) and 85th Foot (1793). The Durham Light Infantry from 68th Foot (1756) and 106th Foot (1839). The Royal Green Jackets (1966) from The Oxfordshire and Buckinghamshire Light Infantry (1908), formerly The Oxfordshire Light Infantry (1881), The King's Royal Rifle Corps (1755), formerly 60th Foot, and The Rifle Brigade (Prince Consort's Own) (1800), formerly 95th Foot. The Oxfordshire and Buckinghamshire Light Infantry from 43rd Foot (1741) and 52nd Foot (1755).

Corps of Royal Marines (1755).

The Parachute Regiment (1940).

The Brigade of Gurkhas comprises:

1. **The 1st Royal Gurkha Regiment** (1994) from 2nd King Edward VII's Own Goorkha Rifles (The Sirmoor Rifles) (1815) and 6th Queen Elizabeth's Own Gurkha Rifles (1817).

2. **The 2nd Royal Gurkha Regiment** (1996) from 2nd Royal Gurkha Regiment (1994), formerly 7th Duke of Edinburgh's Own Gurkha Rifles (1902), and 3rd Royal Gurkha Regiment (1994), formerly 10th Princess Mary's Own Gurkha Rifles (1887).
3. **Queen's Gurkha Engineers** (1955).

4. **Queen's Gurkha Signals** (1955).

5. **Gurkha Transport Regiment** (1965), formerly Gurkha Army Service Corps (1958).

22nd Special Air Service Regiment (1952).

Army Air Corps (1942).

Royal Army Chaplains' Department (1919), formerly Army Chaplains' Department (1796).

Royal Logistic Corps (1993) from Royal Corps of Transport (1965), Royal Army Ordnance Corps (1875), Royal Pioneer Corps (1939), Army Catering Corps (1941) and Royal Engineers (Postal and Courier Service) (1913). RCT from Royal Army Service Corps (1888).

Royal Electrical and Mechanical Engineers (1942).

The Adjutant General's Corps (1992) from Royal Military Police (1877), Military Provost Staff Corps (1901), Royal Army Pay Corps (1878), Royal Army Educational Corps (1920), Women's Royal Army Corps (1949), and Army Legal Corps (1978).

Royal Army Veterinary Corps (1881).

Small Arms School Corps (1929).

Royal Army Dental Corps (1921).

Intelligence Corps (1940).

Army Physical Training Corps (1940).

Queen Alexandra's Royal Army Nursing Corps (1949) from The Army Nursing Service (1897).

The Gibraltar Regiment (1958), formerly Gibraltar Defence Force (1939).

A Daimler Armoured Car Mark 1 outside 'Horse Power', the museum of The King's Royal Hussars at Winchester.

Appendix III:
Regimental lineage of disbanded regiments

The Royal Irish Regiment (1881), formerly 18th Foot (1684). Disbanded 1922.

The Cameronians (Scottish Rifles) (1881), from 26th Foot (1689) and 90th Foot (1794). Disbanded 1968.

The York and Lancaster Regiment (1881), from 65th Foot (1756) and 84th Foot (1793). Disbanded 1968.

The Connaught Rangers (1881), from 88th Foot (1793) and 94th Foot (1823). Disbanded 1922.

The Prince of Wales's Leinster Regiment (Royal Canadians) (1881), from 100th Foot (1858) and 109th Foot (1859). Disbanded 1922.

The Royal Munster Fusiliers (1881), from 101st Foot (1652) and 104th Foot (1839). Disbanded 1922.

The Royal Dublin Fusiliers (1881), from 102nd Foot (1641) and 103rd Foot (1662). Disbanded 1922.

A window in the Chapel of St George in Sheffield Cathedral commemorates the 65th Foot, part of the disbanded York and Lancaster Regiment.

Bibliography

GENERAL

Anglesey, Marquess of. *A History of the British Cavalry* (eight volumes). Leo Cooper, London, 1973-1997.

Barnett, Corelli. *Britain and Her Army, 1509-1970*. Allen Lane, London, 1970.

Beckett, Ian. *The Amateur Military Tradition, 1558-1945*. Manchester University Press, Manchester, 1991.

Carver, Michael. *The Seven Ages of the British Army*. Weidenfeld & Nicolson, London, 1984.

Chandler, David, and Beckett, Ian (editors). *The Oxford Illustrated History of the British Army*. Oxford University Press, Oxford, 1994.

Fortescue, Sir John. *The History of the British Army* (thirteen volumes). Macmillan, London, 1899-1930.

French, David. *The British Way in Warfare, 1688-2000*. Allen & Unwin, London, 1990.

Heathcote, Tony. *The Military in British India*. Manchester University Press, Manchester, 1995.

Strachan, Hew. *The Politics of the British Army*. Clarendon Press, Oxford, 1997.

White, A.S. *A Bibliography of Regimental Histories of the British Army*. Society for Army Historical Research, London, 1965.

PARTICULAR PERIODS

Beckett, Ian, and Simpson, Keith (editors). *A Nation in Arms: A Social Study of the British Army in the First World War*. Manchester University Press, Manchester, 1985.

Beckett, Ian. *The Army and the Curragh Incident, 1914*. Bodley Head, London, 1986.

Bond, Brian (editor). *Victorian Military Campaigns*. Hutchinson, London, 1967.

Bond, Brian. *British Military Policy between the Two World Wars*. Clarendon Press, Oxford, 1980.

Bond, Brian (editor). *The First World War and British Military History*. Clarendon Press, Oxford, 1991.

Childs, John. *The Army of Charles II*. Routledge & Kegan Paul, London, 1976.

Childs, John. *The Army, James II and the Glorious Revolution*. Manchester University Press, Manchester, 1980.

Childs, John. *The British Army of William III, 1689-1702*. Manchester University Press, Manchester, 1987.

Fraser, David. *And We Shall Shock Them: The British Army in the Second World War.* Hodder & Stoughton, London, 1983.

French, David. *Military Identities: The Regimental System, the British Army, and the British People, 1870–2000.* Oxford University Press, Oxford, 2005.

Gentles, Ian. *The New Model Army in England, Ireland and Scotland, 1645-1653.* Clarendon Press, Oxford, 1991.

Glover, Richard. *Peninsular Preparation: The Reform of the British Army, 1795-1809.* Cambridge University Press, Cambridge, 1963.

Gooch, John. *The Plans of War: The General Staff and British Military Strategy, 1900-1916.* Routledge & Kegan Paul, London, 1974.

Guy, Alan. *Oeconomy and Discipline: Officership and Administration in the British Army, 1714-1783.* Manchester University Press, Manchester, 1984.

Guy, Alan (editor). *The Road to Waterloo.* National Army Museum, London, 1990.

Hamer, W.S. *The British Army: Civil-Military Relations, 1885-1905.* Clarendon Press, Oxford, 1970.

Hayter, Tony. *The Army and the Crowd in Mid-Georgian England.* Macmillan, London, 1978.

Houlding, John. *Fit for Service: The Training of the British Army, 1715-1795.* Clarendon Press, Oxford, 1981.

Jeffery, Keith. *The British Army and the Crisis of Empire, 1918-1922.* Manchester University Press, Manchester, 1984.

Knight, Ian. *Go to Your God Like a Soldier: The British Soldier Fighting for Empire, 1837-1902.* Greenhill Books, London, 1996.

Mackesy, Piers. *The War for America, 1775-1783.* Harvard University Press, Cambridge, Ma, 1964.

Mackesy, Piers. *British Victory in Egypt, 1801.* Routledge, London, 1995.

Mockaitis, Thomas. *British Counter-insurgency, 1919-1960.* Macmillan, London, 1990.

Mockaitis, Thomas. *British Counter-insurgency in the Post-imperial Era.* Manchester University Press, Manchester, 1995.

Pimlott, John (editor). *British Military Operations, 1945-1984.* Hamlyn/Bison, London, 1984.

Savory, Sir Reginald. *His Britannic Majesty's Army in Germany during the Seven Years' War.* Clarendon Press, Oxford, 1966.

Scouller, R.E. *The Armies of Queen Anne.* Clarendon Press, Oxford, 1960.

Simkins, Peter. *Kitchener's Army: The Raising of the New Armies, 1914-1916.* Manchester University Press, Manchester, 1988.

Skelley, A.R. *The Victorian Army at Home*. Croom Helm, London, 1977.

Spiers, Edward. *The Army and Society, 1815-1914*. Longman, London, 1980.

Spiers, Edward. *The Late Victorian Army, 1868-1902*. Manchester University Press, Manchester, 1992.

Strachan, Hew. *Wellington's Legacy: The Reform of the British Army, 1830-1854*. Manchester University Press, Manchester, 1984.

Strachan, Hew. *From Waterloo to Balaclava: Tactics, Technology, and the British Army, 1815-1854*. Cambridge University Press, Cambridge, 1985.

Travers, Tim. *The Killing Ground: The British Army, the Western Front and the Emergence of Modern Warfare, 1900-1918*. Unwin Hyman, London, 1987.

Travers, Tim. *How the War Was Won: Command and Technology in the British Army on the Western Front, 1917-1918*. Routledge, London, 1992.

TRADITIONS, CUSTOMS AND UNIFORMS

Edwards, T.J. *Military Customs*. Gale & Polden, Aldershot, 1950.

Edwards, T.J. *Regimental Badges*. Gale & Polden, Aldershot, 1951.

Edwards, T.J. *Mascots and Pets of the Services*. Gale & Polden, Aldershot, 1953.

Edwards, T.J. *Standards, Guidons and Colours of the Commonwealth Forces*. Gale & Polden, Aldershot, 1953.

Hallows, Ian. *Regiments and Corps of the British Army*. Arms and Armour Press, London, 1991.

Leslie, N.B. *Battle Honours of the British and Indian Armies, 1695-1914*. London, 1970.

Smith, D.J. *Discovering Horse-Drawn Transport of the British Army*. Shire, Princes Risborough, 1977.

Taylor, Arthur. *Discovering English County Regiments*. Shire, Princes Risborough, second edition 1987.

Taylor, Arthur. *Discovering Military Traditions*. Shire, Aylesbury, second edition 1972.

Taylor, Arthur. *Discovering British Military Uniforms*. Shire, Princes Risborough, 1972 (reprinted 1987).

Taylor, Arthur. *Discovering British Cavalry Regiments*. Shire, Aylesbury, 1973.

MILITARY GENEALOGY

Farrington, Anthony. *Guide to the Records of the India Office Military Department*. India Office Library, London, 1982.

Fowler, Simon. *Army Records for Family Historians*. Public Record Office, Kew, 1992.

Fowler, Simon; Spencer, William, and Tamblin, Simon. *Army Service Records of the First World War*. Public Record Office, Kew, 1997.

Gibson, Jeremy, and Medlycott, Mervyn. *Militia Lists and Musters, 1757-1876*. Federation of Family History Societies, Birmingham, 1990.

Hamilton-Edwards, Gerald. *In Search of Army Ancestry*. Phillimore, Chichester, 1977.

Holding, Norman. *World War One Army Ancestry*. Federation of Family History Societies, Birmingham, 1991.

McIntyre, Colin, *Monuments of War: How to Read a War Memorial*. Robert Hale, London, 1990.

Roper, Michael. *The Records of the War Office and Related Departments, 1660-1964*. Public Record Office, Kew, 1998.

Spencer, William. *Records of the Militia and Volunteer Forces, 1757-1945*. Public Record Office, Kew, 1997.

Thomas, Gareth. *Records of the Royal Marines*. Public Record Office, Kew, 1994.

Watts, Michael, and Watts, Christopher. *My Ancestor Was in the British Army*. Society of Genealogists, London, 1992.

MILITARY SITES

Boorman, Derek. *At the Going Down of the Sun: British First World War Memorials*. Dunnington, York, 1988.

Boorman, Derek. *For Your Tomorrow: British Second World War Memorials*. Dunnington, York, 1995.

Douet, James. *British Barracks, 1600-1914: Their Architecture and Role in Society*. English Heritage, London, 1998.

Kinross, John. *Discovering Battlefields of England and Scotland*. Shire Publications, Princes Risborough, 1998; reprinted 2004.

Saunders, Andrew. *Fortress Britain: Artillery Fortification in the British Isles and Ireland*. Beaufort Publishing, Liphook, 1989.

Save Britain's Heritage. *Deserted Bastions: Historic Naval and Military Architecture*. SAVE, London, 1993.

Smurthwaite, David. *The Complete Guide to Battlefields in Britain*. Michael Joseph, London, 1993.

Wills, H. *Pillboxes: A Study of UK Defences*. Leo Cooper, London, 1985.

Useful addresses

Army Records Society, c/o National Army Museum, Royal Hospital Road, Chelsea, London SW3 4HT. Website: www.armyrecordssociety.org.uk (Publishes annual volume of historical documents.)

The Battlefields Trust, c/o Meadow Cottage, 33 High Green, Brooke, Norwich NR15 1HR. Website: www.battlefieldstrust.com (Regular newsletter, visits and conferences.)

The Commonwealth War Graves Commission, 2 Marlow Road, Maidenhead, Berkshire SL6 7DX. Telephone: 01628 634221. Website: www.cwgc.org

Military Historical Society, c/o National Army Museum, Royal Hospital Road, Chelsea, London SW3 4HT. Website: www.army.mod.uk/contacts/divisions/history.htm or www.national-army-museum.ac.uk (Publishes quarterly bulletin, mostly on uniforms and badges.)

Society for Army Historical Research, c/o National Army Museum, Royal Hospital Road, Chelsea, London SW3 4HT. Website: www.sahr.co.uk or www.national-army-museum.co.uk (Publishes quarterly journal.)

Victorian Military Society, PO Box 5837, Newbury, Berkshire RG14 7FJ. Website: www.victorianmilitarysociety.org.uk (Publishes quarterly journal, *Soldiers of the Queen.*)

War Memorials Trust, c/o 4 Lower Belgrave Street, London SW1W 0LA. Telephone: 020 7881 0862. Website: www.warmemorials.org (Newsletters.)

Western Front Association, c/o Potters Lodge, Bassetsbury Lane, High Wycombe, Buckinghamshire HP11 1QU. Website: www.westernfront.co.uk (Publishes quarterly journal, *Stand To.)*

A commemorative plate dating from 1899 and bearing a portrait of the British commander in chief during the second phase of the South African War, Field Marshal Earl Roberts, VC. Roberts had won his VC in the Indian Mutiny.

Index